NATIONAL SECURITY IN PERSPECTIVE

NATIONAL SECURITY IN PERSPECTIVE

Dr. S.T. DAS

Gian Publishing House

29/6 SHAKTI NAGAR • DELHI-110007 • INDIA

GIAN PUBLISHING HOUSE
29/6 Shakti Nagar, Delhi-110007

ISBN 81-212– 0102-0

PRINTED IN INDIA

Published by Gian Publishing House, Delhi (India) and
Printed at Mohan Printing Corporation
(Composing at Godwall Printers), Delhi.

PREFACE

To appreciate the importance of national security, the students should realise that there is strong relationship between geography and world problems. He should see that the historic struggle for power among nations and people cannot be interpreted without the help of geography and that geographic considerations, in their broadest sense, are the cause of most wars Geography is an integral part of the planining of war on land and seas.

To direct military planning, to participate actively in a war or even to understand military strategy and tacties, one must know the effects of geographical forces on military opeartions. A conventional war and perhaps even space-age wars can not be planned or waged without intimate knowledge of climate, weather, topography and ground cover ; the width, depth and navigability of rivers ; the size and shape of occans and adjoining seas ; the existence of life lines ; the shape, area and relative locations of the continents, countries and islands, distribution of arable land, minerals, natural resources and manufacturing centres.

The power of a nation is conditioned by (1) what that nation is in relation to people and national consciousness, (2) what it has in land and material resources. Under material resources are classified all those material things needed for maintaining a peacetime economic and for waging war.

By total power potentail is meant all the human and material resources that a state can draw upon once it has completed its mobilization and organization for war. That part of its resources which a state can convert immediately into military power, is its effective power potential.

Although an adequate supply of minerals and metals is ab solutely essential in conducting modern warfare, there must, in addition, be adequate supplies of food and plenty of labour to do the work of preparing for and maintaining active effort.

Most of the chapters in this book are studies of the bases of power, but it is also possible and desirable for the reader to evaluate the present and potential power of the significant national states.

I make no claim as to the originality of subject-matter of the book. I believe the arrangement and presentation of the book is novel and unique.

In a book like this, I must acknowledge the assistance I have received from various authorities, who offered valuable help and those whose works have helped me to draw inspiration to complete the project.

I am grateful to my daughters Kumari Nivedita and Sunandita, who cheered me up to maintain the tempo of writing despite many difficulties. Last but not least, my intellectual and mental love to my wife Mina, without whose help, cooperation and inspiration, this book would not have seen the hight of the day.

S.T. Das.

133-E
Kamla Nagar
Delhi-7

CONTENTS

INTRODUCTION

This book is designed to acquaint readers with the major regional facts and principles which contribute to a nation's development, power and policies, and upon which many aspects of strategy are based. The majority of the chapters in this book are studies of the bases of power but it is also possible and desirable for the reader to evaluate the present and potential power of the significant national states.

The geo-strategy may be defined concisely as the science of geopolitics that deals with strategy ; the combination of geography and world problems along with strategic factors characterizing a particular geographic region.

Geography may be defined concisely as the science of the earth and its life. More explicitly, the science of geography deals with the surface of the earth ; its division into regions, continents and countries ; and the climate, plants, animals, natural resources, inhabitants and industries of the various divisions. In its fullest sense, therefore, geography is almost unlimited in scope. Geography may be studied either in its broad context or it may be divided into physical, economic, human and political geography. In analysing the relationship between geography, power and strategy, this book uses the broad interpretation of geo-strategy.

To appreciate the science of geography, the readers should realize that there is a strong relationship between geography and world problems. He should see that the historic struggle for power among nations and peoples cannot be interpreted without the help of geography, and that geographic considerations, in their broadest sense, are the cause of most wars. He should understand that geography is an integral part of the planning of war on land and sea. It should become obvious to him that the men who might devise a political system to prevent war, will need a complete understanding of geography in its relation to human affairs. Only by a knowledge of "global geography," wherein one can sense the world as a unit, is one capable of appreciating the relationship between geography, power and strategy. (From these premises should grow a new understanding of the importance of this subject and a will to master its lessons.)

To direct military planning, to participate actively in a war or even to understand military strategy and tactics, one must know the effects of geographical forces on military operations. A conventional war and perhaps even space-age wars, cannot be planned or waged without intimate knowledge of climate, weather, topography and ground cover ; the width, depth and navigability of rivers ; the size and shape of oceans and adjoining seas ; the existence of life lines and navigational hazards, the shape, area and relative locations of the continents, countries and islands ; characteristics of the coastlines ; and the distribution of arable land, manufacturing centres and natural resources. Actually, these are only a few of the geographical facts which military strategists must take into account. Although political and military leaders have paid lip service to geography for centuries, they have not always learned its lessons or, more significantly, applied them.

It is not the purpose of this study to give the reader a thorough schooling in geography, strategy or geopolitics. It is intended to give him a new appreciation of the science of geography and some understanding of geography as the basis of power and power politics. This book should help one to gain a better insight into India's position in world affairs and a sounder basis for thought about the course that India must chart in order to maintain that position. And, finally, it should point out the geographic considerations essential for a comprehension of the problems of strategy.

Before proceeding further, it is well to consider certain important terms and their use in this study :

Geopolitics : This is the science of the relation of politics to geography. The subject matter of geopolitics is derived from political geography, history, imperialism and military, naval and air strategy. Geo-politicians contend that the strength of a nation and its chances for survival depend, to a great extent, on geographical factors—location and manpower, natural resources, industrial capacity and social and political organization. In addition, geo-politicians contend that by examining these conditions in a specific nation, the future of that nation can be charted. Even if one does not accept all the conclusions of the geo-politicians, they do have a firm foundation in historical fact. Naked power has always been a vital force in world history, and power rests securely upon geographical foundations.

Elements of Power : The power of a nation is conditioned by (1) what that nation is in relation to people and national consciousness, and (2) what it has in land and material resources. Human resources include not only manpower but also those characteristics required to make manpower effective : "know-how," national cohesion, energy, resourcefulness and character, type and influence of the government. Under material resources are classified all those material things needed for maintaining a peacetime economy and for waging war. Among these resources are transportation and industrial systems as well as natural resources from which a modern war machine is built and upon which it is run. From a study of itself and other countries in regard to all these elements, a nation can arrive at conclusions, necessarily rough and tentative, upon which to base its foreign policy.

Total and Effective Power Potential : By total power potential is meant all the human and material resources that a state can draw upon once it has completed its mobilization and organization for war. That part of its resources which a state can convert immediately into military power, is its effective power potential. America's war with Japan illustrates this distinction perfectly, for the USA and Japan were almost opposite extremes in both total effective potential. The USA, with its tremendous total potential, was unprepared for a global war or even defence of its own shores. Japan, although low in total potential, had been able by planning and organization to build up its effective potential to the point that it dared make the attack on Pearl Harbour. The outcome proved beyond doubt the long-range superiority of a high total potential over a high effective potential. There is considerable doubt today, however, that in a future war, any nation will have the opportunity and time that the USA had to build up its effective potential.

National Policy : The power of a national state is measured by the degree to which it is able to achieve that which it desires. The sum of the desires or objectives of a nation is known as the national interest. The means that the government pursues to attain these ends are termed national policy—domestic policy so far as it relates to affairs within, and foreign policy as it relates to affairs outside the nation. The soundness of a national policy in peace time may be measured by the success with which it uses the nation's resources and energies to provide prosperity, amicable foreign relations and the safeguards of defence.

A nation may implement its foreign policy by several means including the common ones of negotiation, propaganda, economic power and military force. Negotiation or diplomacy is the first means a state employs to execute its foreign policies to obtain allies and to protect itself. In a cold war particularly, the use of propaganda and economic power can be very effective. Normally, actual war is used by a state as a last resort, after diplomacy has failed, to promote its national security. War itself is of two types, defensive and aggressive. Each requires full knowledge and use of geography.

Strategy : In a technical or military sense, strategy involves deciding upon the geographic area(s) of military operations, the planning for, and the directing of the military forces to be employed therein. Strategy should not be confused with tactics, which is the manoeuvring of forces in actual contact with the enemy. A major objective of the present study is to consider geographical knowledge that is essential for the planning of effective strategy in the significant areas of the world. A strategic position implies one that is favourable or advantageous primarily because of geographical location. The evaluation of the strategic position of nations and of regions, based upon geographic and economic factors, will be stressed in the following pages.

In each of the chapters of this book, there is an analysis of the many and varied considerations involved in the defence of the various areas of the world. The question of defence has always been important ; today, for actual survival, it is vital.

OCEAN AREAS

The oceans are an important phase of man's study of the world around him not only because of their vast size but also because of the direct influences which they have upon man's many activities. We find it difficult to realize that three-fourths of the earth's surface are covered by water. The five major oceans—Atlantic, Pacific, Indian, Arctic and Antarctic—cover 141 million square miles. The Polar seas alone contain some 11 million square miles, which have comparatively little commercial value but the Arctic, particularly, may be of great military consequence in the future.

Although oceans act as barriers and separate the inhabitants of continents and islands, they serve simultaneously as avenues of communication between the land areas. An ocean is a defensive buffer for a state ; it is also a carrier of military personnel and equipment for offensive warfare. In addition, the oceans have significant economic value because of their plant, animal and even mineral resources and because they are highways for importing needed articles and for exporting surplus goods. Peacetime commerce and wartime logistics alike make cheap and efficient use of the world's waterways. Indeed 90 per cent of the world's commerce is carried by water. The oceans, therefore, figure strongly in a nation's warfare, its commerce, its climate and its contacts with the political and cultural institutions of other states. Because of this fact, history is filled with the competition of nations for access to the sea and for control of the seas.

In studying an ocean, its position upon the earth's surface and the extent and character of the lands bordering it must be ascertained. Just as the location of a river can be significant because of the population or manufacturing centres that it joins together, so is the location of an ocean important. In fact, favourable location of a particular ocean can be its most significant feature. This condition may be caused by its position in regard to world trade and its bordering lands, its access to other waterways, its effects upon climate, its availability for peaceful contacts or for military expeditions, or its use for economic or even recreational purposes. In reverse, sea frontage of a nation may be a most significant feature of its physical location. Obviously, the location of some oceans has a much greater effect than that of others ; one can hardly compare the importance of the Antarctic Ocean with that of the Atlantic Ocean or the Indian ocean for example.

SIZE AND SHAPE

The size and shape of an ocean may well affect its economic and strategic importance. Shape is of lesser importance but is one of the determinants in the evaluation of an ocean area. Size, however, determines the climatic belts spanned by an ocean and the amount of bordering land and population. Size can be either an asset or a handicap, depending upon the distances involved in traversing the ocean. The vast Pacific contains almost half the ocean area of the world. The distances to be travelled in that ocean area tremendous whereas in the North Atlantic, a ship is never more than 1,500 miles from a coastline.

OCEANOGRAPHY

To know an ocean in a physical sense, one must be familiar with its currents, tides and winds ; its islands and island chains ; and its hazards to navigation, including storms, ice patterns and reefs. Such knowledge is of the utmost importance to a navigator whether he be involved in military or commercial activity, and to any strategic planning for the use of the oceans. This study emphasizes, therefore, those characteristics of an ocean that pertain primarily to its physical geography and that bear most directly upon its economic and strategic significance rather than the more scientific aspects of oceanography.

Other than as media of transportation, oceans are of tremendous importance to the economy of the world. Fishing for food as well as such specialized types of fishing as for pearls, coral and sponges, affords an occupation to many individuals and is an important aspect of the economy of some nations. Whaling and sealing and their by-products contribute to some national economies and the mineral resources of the oceans are becoming increasingly important. Sea frontage is, of course, a strong influence in stimulating nations to engage in shipbuilding. All maritime states support this industry to some extent ; in some it is a large and basic industry.

In a general sense, man's greatest use of the oceans lies in the field of transportation, and ships remain the most economical and efficient media of transportation. In analysing the trade potentialities of the oceans, this study will emphasize the routes, volume and value of trade of the ocean areas. In addition, there will be an indication of the economic importance of the bordering lands wherever it is pertinent. Since approximately 90 per cent of the world's trade is carried by water, without such a medium the economy and standard of living of practically every nation would be affected adversely. No nation can hope to be self-sufficient ; every nation must engage in some international trade for essential or desired products that it does not possess.

CRITICAL AREAS

Along the coastlines of practically every ocean, there exist land areas that are critical in a political sense because of an actual or a potential contest for control or ownership of these areas. Such a contest could be the result of one or more desires or demands : sea frontage and harbours, natural resources, strategic locations, bases, outlets for excess population or even expansion of ideologies. The reader will see that some of the critical areas have been so characterized for many years : others have only recently reached the critical status. As new states industrialize, additional resources begin to become strategic, or as the ideological fight continues and expands, additional areas will undoubtedly become critical. This development will be the case particularly as attempts are made to bring more states under communist domination.

LIFE LINES

To a great extent, ocean life lines follow the normal trade routes. They are significant in both peacetime and wartime. They are of greatest importance during wartime, especially when a nation is fighting for its very existence and must rely upon control of the seas and upon keeping its life lines open in order to survive. Nor are usable life lines a necessity only for the home state ; they are also a pre-requisite for the effective logistic support of advanced bases and of military forces operating overseas. Even in the "Atomic Age," a primary responsibility of naval forces is to keep open the life lines which provide a means for supplying the home countries and advanced bases with strategic products. Failure to fulfil this responsibility would result in a reduced standard of living and, in wartime, possible defeat.

BASES

In the consideration of strategy and strategic movements, the presence of advanced bases for operations and for logistic maintenance and support are of the utmost importance. This old axiom is as valid for today and for future wars as for the past. The location of these bases is one of their most significant characteristics – location with respect to the home country as well as to the battle area. Each of the world's oceans contains bases ; some have more than others. And, of course, some of the bases are of infinitely greater importance than others, primarily because of their strategic location in respect of a prospective area of warfare. The USA undoubtedly has built up the greatest system of bases throughout the world. Some locations, such as the Panama and Suez canals, have a peculiar significance because of their effect upon logistics. Furthermore, some of the world's gateways or bottlenecks between oceans, most of which belong to the British Commonwealth, continue to be of great importance because of the lasting need for control of the seas.

COMMUNICATIONS

Communications have always been a fundamental problem to man in time of both peace and war. They have, of course, been a more acute problem in wartime and have, perhaps, faced a greater challenge in the vast distances of the ocean areas. The more effective the communications, the greater is man's mastery over time and distance. Today, with fast ships, airplanes, radio, telephones and cables and with technical advances in electronics, the basic problems posed by the question of communications have been solved. This fact does not imply, however, that there is no room for improvement or that the nations do not have to maintain their communications systems at the peak of effectiveness. It is well recognized today that a breakdown in communications could result in disaster.

DEFENCE STRATEGY

1. *Time and Distance Factors* : That the world has shrunk in terms of time and miles, is well known. The Air Age has made the old problem of time and distance only a relative one in terms of hours. Despite this fact, time and distance in the ocean areas continue to be fundamental questions when determining defence strategy. In a sense, they have become even more acute because of the fact that now defenders must make decisions based upon the consideration of hours or even minutes, rather than days. In this study, attempts are made to familiarize the reader with the most significant time-distance factors of the ocean areas in terms of both air and sea travel.

2. *Challengers and Contestants* : In general, one might say that in each of the ocean areas, the contestants are the communist countries and the other democracies or, to be more

specific, the USA and the USSR. The challengers in each of the ocean areas are motivated by a variety of factors and have objectives that differ in nature and degree. The defenders would, of course, contest such challengers because their own possessions, economy or sense of security would be adversely affected.

CHAPTER ONE

FACTORS OF GEO-STRATEGY

How does one go about the complex task of evaluating the power potential of a region or of a nation? How does one undertake an appraisal of an ocean area for the purpose of estimating its commercial potentialities or of planning offensive or defensive strategy? What are the points that must be considered, the questions that must be asked, in order to arrive at an evaluation or an appraisal?

These questions illustrate the complex nature of making geo-political assessments. The purposes of this chapter are to provide guidelines for analysing the power potential and to point out the defensive considerations in the significant regions and major powers of the world. One should be able to make a meaningful evaluation of nations and regions by applying to them the principles discussed in the section on land areas. Moreover, one can also arrive at significant conclusions regarding the use—military and strategic—of oceans by studying them according to the format established in this chapter.

LAND AREAS

Location : Location is obviously an important factor in the development of power, for it can determine climates, economies and even national policies. Moreover, tremendous economic and strategic advantages can result from favourable geographical location. These advantages accrue either because the location in itself has strategic value, or because of its proximity to trade routes, other countries, population centres or vital areas. Location is particularly important in the diplomacy and strategy of war.

Many countries illustrate the significant effects of geographical location. The position of the British Isles athwart the trade routes to and from Western Europe, for example, has contributed greatly to the commercial development of the United Kingdom. The United States occupies an advantageous position as a terminus of the trade routes of both the Atlantic and Pacific. In the same way, India occupies an advantageous position in Asia. The position of India athwart to trade routes from east to west. Moreover, with weak and friendly neighbours on its borders and large water areas separating it from Europe and Asia, the United States was able in the past to shape its national policy in comparative freedom from external pressures.

Size, Shape and Depth : Size in itself is not a determinant of power ; many other elements must be combined to assure a nation's strength and effectiveness. There are several possible advantages, however, that a large country may enjoy—among them, variety of climate, ample arable land, varied natural resources, large population and greater defence in depth from attack. On the other hand, large size can be over-emphasized or can actually constitute a disadvantage. For example, Brazil and China, each larger than the USA, contain vast areas of wasteland ; and the Soviet Union has an area larger than the United States that is almost constantly frozen. Moreover, great size can complicate the problems of defence, national unity and effective administration So far as India's size is concerned, it is easily accessible to all direction in all weather, except in the mountainous north which is frozen for three months.

Shape is another important consideration in the political and economic life of a nation and its military policies. Compactness, such as exists in France and Spain, fosters political unity. It facilitates political administration and the speedy mobilization of military forces, labour and industry. On the other hand, compactness, such as in Belgium, can be a liability since it is susceptible to attack, particularly from the air. If a country is excessively elongated like Chile, Norway and Italy, or if its area is separated, like that of Turkey and the USA, its vulnerability to invasion is increased. Moreover, such countries often have to contend with pronounced regionalism which is a barrier to national unity.

Depth is derived primarily from size and secondarily from shape and has always been important in the defence capabilities of a country. In a sense, depth may also be provided by ocean frontiers which can act as a buffer or cushion for a nation threatened with invasion.

The USSR, India and the USA are three excellent examples of countries blessed with both great size and depth. Unfortunately, the USA has large concentrations of industry along her vulnerable coastlines and, in addition, has Alaska and Hawaii to consider. During World War II, the Soviet Union used its depth by withdrawing into the interior and scorching the earth behind its retreating forces thus causing the Nazis to over-extend their supply lines dangerously. On the other hand, although sheer space acts as a defence against invasion, we should bear in mind also that depth can work to the advantage of defender and attacker alike since military operations over large distances are extremely difficult.

Weather and Climate : Climate conditions, the health and energy of man ; it determines the nature and distribution of the food supply ; and it influences man's very living habits. All of the world's great powers lie in the middle latitudes, in which variations in climate and soil are not too great. Two types of climate are characteristic of these areas : oceanic and continental. Oceanic climates, with mild winters and cool summers, prevail along the western margins of the continents in the Northern Hemisphere ; the continental climates, with greater extremes of heat and cold, are found on the eastern coasts and in the interior. Nations large in area, such as India and the USA, benefit from the fact that they include within their boundaries climates of differing types which contribute to the variety and balance of productive capacities.

Extreme cold, dryness or heat creates problems which no country has been able to solve. Wherever the climate is too hot, too rainy or too cold, we find little national progress. Agricultural production in quantities sufficient to support a large population is impossible in frigid or arid areas 30 to 50 inches of annual rainfall is the optimum in agricultural; the minimum for productivity is 20 inches. In those places near the Equator where extreme heat and heavy rainfall are the rule, the heat and humidity enervate the people ; and although vegetable and animal life abounds, the development of natural resources in tropical areas has been retarded greatly. Similarly, in frigid zones, the intense cold absorbs so much human energy that there is little left for productive purposes.

Physiography : In evaluating nations or regions, one must consider their general physiography—the highlands, lowlands, coastlines, plains, forests, swamps and cultivated areas. Topography is of the utmost importance in the determination of offensive or defensive strategy. Often the physiography of an area plays a vital role either in unifying it for strength or in subdividing it for weakness.

Every country contains areas whose physical characteristics, whether of terrain, resources or climate, favour economic progress and growth of population as well as other regions in which such progress and growth are retarded or prevented. In general, the more favoured areas are those having productive soils or mineral resources or both, combined with a terrain that does not offer serious obstacles to the movement of people and goods.

Manpower : Without adequate manpower, no nation can aspire to greatness, for manpower is a necessity for the farms, factories and armed forces. In India, the USA, Germany, the United Kingdom and other nations, an increase in the birth rate was an important factor in their rise to power. It is noteworthy that where nations are more or less equal in industrialization and output per worker, a surplus in manpower may be the decisive advantage in their power relationships.

A large population in itself, however, cannot guarantee power ; for without natural resources, industrial "knowhow" and national unity, it may be an actual weakness. The hundreds of millions of people in the subcontinent of India, for example, are not in themselves a determinant of power. In fact, too large a population may result in a lowered standard of living, reduced efficiency and possibly even national weakness.

Population density is measured by dividing the number of inhabitants by the total area. This figure can be misleading, however, for it does not take into consideration the uneven distribution of population within the country. For example, China, with a relatively low density figure, has vast areas in the interior that will not sustain large populations. This condition results in extreme crowding in the productive coastal regions. To determine whether a country could support more people at an equal or higher standard of living, it is necessary to go beyond the density figure and consider the facts of the physical geography of that nation.

Population Trends : Modern war demands huge numbers of people not only in uniform but also on the home front to feed, equip and supply the nation. For this reason, leaders of a state must know the population trends of their own and of other countries. One important consideration is the relative rate of population increase ; another is the age grouping of the population. In arriving at their conclusions regarding population, the experts use the term net rate of reproduction--the ratio of actual births to the births that would be necessary to maintain that population at a static level.

In certain areas, very definite population trends are developing. Inasmuch as population increases, other than the so-called population explosions, indicate potential power and a decline has always resulted in a corresponding loss of power, one must be seriously concerned with these trends.

The populations of the USSR, India, Latin America and the Far East, as well as the Latin and Slavic areas of Europe, are growing rapidly. Their rates of reproduction are increasing and their mortality rates are decreasing. Until recently the rate of population increase in the USA since World War II had been greater than the experts had predicted. On the other hand, the populations of most of the nations of north-western Europe are decreasing. In France, where the birth rate has been declining since 1935, the situation has been causing alarm.

Characteristics : Some nations, like people, have distinguishing traits or characteristics. The British, for example, possess a greater measure of political genius perhaps than any other large group of people since ancient Rome, and along with Rome, are recognized as superior lawmakers. The Germans have shown themselves to be devotees of education, scientific investigation and efficient methods ; and they are also noted for thrift and industriousness. A national characteristic that is common to both Germany and Japan is obedience to authority or control from above.

Cohesion is the ability of the people to work together in pursuit of the national interest in spite of individual or group differences in opinions. This characteristic also involves such considerations as common language, religion, principles of law, relations of labour and capital; class problems and racial differences.

Russia and India furnish excellent examples of the problems that make cohesion difficult. The former has many diverse races and languages. The latter has these divisive factors plus the complications of the caste system and differences between the two major religious groups, Hindus and Muslims.

Standard : For our purposes, we shall limit our definition of standard of living in this study to the materialistic aspects, and not concern ourselves here with the points of ethics, morality and religion. Standard of living might also be called the standard of consumption. This includes such conditions as the quantity and quality of food available to a nation ; the educational, transportation and communication facilities ; the quantity and quality of dwellings ; material goods such as automobiles and labour-saving devices ; and luxuries standards of consumption vary from the high American level to the low Chinese level. In this study, we shall use this term relative to the standard of living in the USA.

BASIC NATURAL RESOURCES

Extensive natural resources and supplies of raw materials are indispensable for political and military power. Of all the natural resources, productive topsoil is the most valuable because its many products are essential for a well-rounded economy. Indeed, without foodstuffs, man cannot survive. Although fertile soil alone is no assurance that a nation possessing it can become a great power, no area completely lacking it has ever become one. An intrinsically fertile soil may be virtually useless, however, if climate or land forms are unfavourable, too cold, too dry, or too rugged.

The importance of minerals has been fully realized only in modern times. In more primitive economics, a large population and fertile soil were the only pre-requisites for a great nation. Today, however, is the age of machines made of, and driven by materials derived almost wholly from mineral resources.

PRODUCTION

(*1*) *Agriculture, forestry and Fishing* : Agricultural and pastoral lands yield vegetable and animal products which feed man and provide much of his clothing, housing and equipment. Because of this fact, every nation bases its economy in the first instance upon agriculture, including the rearing of animals. In the aggregate, farm commodities bulk the largest and have the greatest total value of all classes of goods required by a nation. Part of the United Kingdom's economic difficulties today, for example, is due to her inability to supply her needs in foodstuffs.

Forests are being used in an increasing variety of ways as modern technology converts them into building materials, paper, plastics, clothing and many other products. The importance of forest products is indicated by the emphasis which the USA has been placing on the conservation phase of our reforestation programme.

Oceans yield food and a number of other products, such as whale oil and fertilizers. Recent scientific research shows that the oceans hold untold sources of undeveloped natural resources and wealth. In general, however, ocean products make only a relatively minor contribution to the sum total of a nation's resources. Some nations, such as Japan, do depend to a high degree upon the oceans' yield.

(2) *Mineral and Power Resources* : No nation lacking mineral resources or the access to them, can become a major power, for it is from these resources that man produces weapons, tools, building materials and most other equipment. Mineral resources rank second only to agricultural products as a requirement for national self-sufficiency. Of these minerals, coal, iron ore, petroleum and uranium are the first requisites today.

Steel far outranks all other products derived from mineral resources in general utility and is produced in greater bulk than any but the sum of the building materials. About two tons of iron ore are required to make one ton of steel, but approximately a third of the world's steel is produced from scrap iron rather than from iron prepared especially for that purpose. Steel is composed of iron alloyed with other metals, among which manganese is usually essential. Other metals, notably chromium, nickel, tungsten, molybdenum and vanadium are indispensable in the various kinds of steel used in modern warfare. Although these are strategic materials of prime importance, the world production of the ore of each of them is considerably less than one per cent that of iron ore.

The basic power resources are coal, petroleum, water power and, in the near future, atomic energy. Coal is the most basic fuel and is used primarily as such, but chemical research is constantly finding new uses for it. Oil has been called the "blood stream of modern war," for the battle front and the home front both depend upon oil as a basic fuel. The United States, followed in order by Venezuela and the Soviet Union, is the leading producer of oil. Those nations which have suitable rivers and falls are developing hydroelectric plants. Italy, in particular, with its dearth of mineral fuels, depends on this form of power to an unusual degree. The Soviet Union is blessed with more potential hydroelectric power than any other nation, but as yet, despite great progress, it has not been fully developed.

India is blessed favourably in coal and water. Hence, it has developed thermal and hydroelectric power considerably. It is encouraging to note that due to oil crises, India is developing very fast the solar energy which is in abundance in all weather.

India has every thing necessary to become a great power in near future.

So far as manufacturing for home consumption and export is concerned, India plays an important role in world economy. After producing enough material and food for its own requirement, it is exporting food, machine, technical know-how to other countries.

(3) *Manufacturing* : The degree of productiveness in manufacturing varies sharply among nations. It ranges from the making of simple items for home consumption, through minor export commodities, to the stupendous productive capacity of the United States. Power today is determined largely by a nation's degree of industrialization. The development of manufacturing in a nation, however, depends upon many conditions. Availability of raw materials, the supply and quality of labour and management, transportation and communications, markets, mechanical inventiveness, and capital all contribute to success in manufacturing.

TRANSPORTATION

A well-developed system of interior communications materially enhances commercial prosperity and military potential. Mileage of highways and railroads, their location, the extent of facilities for maintenance and repair, and the quality and amount of rolling stock and other equipment indicate the degree to which a nation is capable of carrying on peacetime commerce or meeting wartime exigencies. Systems of canals, navigable rivers and pipelines supplement other means of transport, particularly in the cheap movement of bulky freight. The strategic location of all internal transportation facilities is of particular importance for both mobilization and defence.

In general, the Western nations have well-developed transportation networks, and paved highways and extensive rail lines are more or less common to most of them. The Soviet Union has made great progress but lack of adequate transportation is still a weakness of that vast nation. China, Latin America and Africa are, on the whole, deficient in adequate railroad and highway networks except in a few areas.

So far as India is concerned, it has developed its rail, road and air communication vastly. Not only this, it has also developed its water transport from one region to another through its rivers.

In almost every country today, the airplane is a vital part of the transportation and communication systems. In areas such as Latin America and China where road and railroad construction is often difficult, air travel is becoming increasingly important for both internal and external transportation.

DEGREE OF SELF-SUFFICIENCY

Self-sufficiency may be described as a nation's ability to sustain itself at a standard of living necessary for the proper physical development of its population without access to outside sources of supply. Since at least 22 industrial raw materials are essential for self-sufficiency, no nation in the world today is completely self-sufficient. Although India, the United States and the Soviet Union come closer to being so in comparison with other nations, there are many commodities which they lack completely or produce in quantities insufficient for their needs.

War introduces another variant in the self-sufficiency problem of a nation. Upon normal peacetime demands of the civilian population, war superimposes the military requirements of the armed forces. Not only is the total output required to meet the demands of modern mechanized warfare greater than that needed for peacetime consumption, but the emphasis shifts sharply into certain specific fields and upon certain articles for which there is the greatest demand -- food, alloys, fuels. There are several ways in which nations attempt to overcome these disadvantages. Stockpiling, substitute materials and new techniques are a few of these means.

OVERSEAS COLONIAL EMPIRES

One of the characteristics of a great power is its control of a large area. The extent and location of colonies and dependencies have been governed largely by the desire to obtain one or all of the following benefits : strategic location for trade or defence, manpower, markets, raw materials, etc. In order to possess these advantages, the major states and many smaller ones have expanded beyond their own borders—even to overseas territories in regions quite remote from the home country.

Contacts and conflicts between the colonies belonging to different nations manifest themselves in the foreign policies of each home country concerned. The more extensive and dispersed a nation's colonies are, the more involved become its relations with other states and the greater are the opportunities for the colonies to participate in the relatively "new nationalism" and to free themselves from the controls of the colonial powers.

Economic Importance : Overseas colonies and dependencies have significance in many other aspects of national life. They are sometimes important source of raw materials. Occasionally they provide markets for finished goods, particularly the products of industry ; but the mere fact that a colony is populous does not guarantee a current market or ensure a future one. The value of a colony as a market is dependent principally upon the level of civilization attained by its inhabitants. Moreover, colonial areas do not necessarily trade in any significant amounts with the mother country.

As for raw materials, colonial territories do not always produce important shares of the world's totals. Notable exceptions have been certain colonies, particularly those of the East Indian areas ; and certain products, such as rubber, tin, vanadium, palm oil and manila-hemp. The fact that colonies ordinarily consume little of what they produce, however, correspondingly increases the worth of their contribution to the commerce and power potential of the home country.

Strategic Importance : In many instances, the principal worth of overseas colonies is in their location. Where strategically situated so as to command broad zones of water or land, or to control vital lines of transportation and communication including air routes, they enhance the power potential of a state by augmenting the pressure it can apply at critical places.

Moreover, they can provide overseas bases of great value in military, naval and air warfare.

Colonies are sometimes attractive as possible sources of manpower for military or industrial purposes. The outstanding example of a nation which sought possessions with this in view was France. Elsewhere colonial areas, especially those which are still sparsely settled, may possibly serve as outlets for excess population.

Overseas territories may contain elements of weakness as well as of strength. For example, trade routes and lines of communication which are long and tenuous must be defended. The colonies themselves look to the homeland for protection even though the colonies' own position may be strategically weak and their borders not readily defensible. Then too, internal troubles in a colony may bring threats of secession. In times of war, all such weaknesses in a nation's colonies must be considered both in dealing with the colonies themselves and with other countries as well. Loss by conquest or by secession is a serious blow not only to the national honour and prestige of the mother country herself but frequently to her strength as a colonial power.

Colonial possessions alter the power position of an imperial nation by modifying its national policy, its defence considerations and its commitments. To maintain its status as a colonial power and to preserve the contribution of its colonies to the national war potential, a nation must be willing and prepared to back its policy and obligations by force.

Strategic Position : Of great importance in determining the strategic position and military potential of a nation are its location with respect to the major land and sea trade routes of the world, its possession of good harbours and the development and extent of its external transportation system. All the major states except the U.S.S.R. occupy favourable positions on the principal ocean routes ; all of them have adequate harbours whether natural or artificial.

A merchant fleet has always been a pre-requisite for a great power and an essential item for any state seeking a well-rounded economy. In fact, the complex economies of today demand even larger merchant fleets than heretofore to facilitate imports and exports. Actual ownership of a merchant marine is not essential, however, since some nations, like Norway, provide carriers for the more heavily industrialized states.

The impact of the Air Age has already had a profound effect upon both the peacetime and wartime economy of the world. Air transport is still in a period of lush growth and is changing and growing so rapidly that about all we know of its future is that it will be marked by steady, occasionally spectacular progress in material equipment and technique, and that this progress will have a tremendous influence on national power. Although most air routes are confined to the major zones of world trade existing today and the bulk of cargo is carried by ship or rail because of the cost factor, we can expect continuing development in the aviation of the future.

FRONTIERS AND CRITICAL AREAS

The entire frontier zone—the marginal areas that surround states on both sides of their land and sea boundaries—is critical strategically. A land frontier is normally made up of a succession of barriers, such as mountains and bodies of water, alternating with gaps, such as plains and rivers. Those gaps which lie directly on avenues of approach towards a country's centres of production are most critical. Coastline frontiers are particularly critical in a strategic or defensive sense ; other areas may be critical because they are the subject of contest between nations. Some areas claim they are important economically ; and still others because they are strategically located.

Perhaps the most critical part of a nation is its core area, for it is the core area that contains the centre of population, political authority and basic sinews of the economic life of the state. Military loss of the core area would normally result in the collapse of national resistance.

DEFENSIVE PLANNING

In planning its defence, a nation must think in terms of invasion, which is actual forcible entry, and attack, which may be merely an assault by bombing planes or bombarding ships. For protection from both invasion and attack, a modern state needs a well balanced defence programme. The old concept—control of the seas and the possession of various outlying bases—is no longer entirely adequate. An army, navy and air force, each with sufficient strength, modern weapons and clearly defined mission, must be maintained. Another important consideration in defence planning is the question of allies—who they are, their location and their reliability. There is more to the strategy of defence, however, than just the number and quality of one's armed forces and those of the allies.

Power politics and national security are based to a great extent upon physical geography and natural resources. In determining and evaluating the many considerations involved in defence, therefore, military leaders must think in terms of geography. The actual physical location of the nation and its outlying possessions, its neighbours and their attitudes, and the proximity of the enemy and his advanced bases are important elements in planning defence. Spatial relationship or the time-distance factor, is always a matter of great concern in strategy in offence, defence and logistic support. The size, shape, depth and general physiography affect greatly the nature of tactics involved as well as defensive strategy. Weather and climate continue to affect land, sea, air and even space warfare.

Defence planning necessarily involves the protection of vital areas. These may be coastlines, land boundaries or population, communication and industrial centres. In defending or attacking a coastline, an exact knowledge of the water area and of the coast is imperative. Coastal areas, by their very nature, may deter or aid amphibious invasion. To protect vital land areas which are vulnerable to the enemy, some nations have created buffer states. The function of such states is to reduce the elements of surprise in a sudden invasion by keeping would be enemies at a greater distance from one's borders. This function has obviously been seriously affected by the potentialities of air attack.

Underlying all else in the problem of defence is the status

of the economic and political strength of the nation and the cohesiveness and determination of its people. A large population in itself does not necessarily constitute strength. What is essential, however, is a sufficiency of people of military and working age who are trained in the art of warfare or in the technique of production.

It should be obvious that a state's success in modern war depends greatly upon its industrial potential. For that matter, economic warfare, in all its aspects, is a prime determinant of success in war. Since no nation can be self-sufficient in the modern complex world, its defence plans must include ways of insuring the constant inflow of those vital raw materials needed by its industrial plant.

One general underlying fact must be understood : defence depends upon no one element ; it is a combination of many. The first line of defence is the military and naval forces but geography—physical, human and economic – is the foundation of a nation and its defence strategy.

CHAPTER TWO

EGO-CENTRICITY AND WORLD POWER

Within the notion of geopolitics falls the broad relationship between geography and foreign relations regardless of whether the latter are static or dynamic. The subject concerns the solutions to the questions of "What difference does it make in foreign policy that a country is in one place instead of another or has one assemblage of environmental characteristics instead of another," and "How can these solutions be best applied to the achievement of national objectives".

These questions relate primarily to spatial relationships, the geometry of the situation and to power potential, all reflecting the environmental elements of the situation. They depend upon broad concepts of distance and accessibility, such as the distribution of continents and oceans or the configuration of the world's coastlines or more narrowly as expressed by landscape formations or atmospheric phenomena. They depend upon the identification and evaluation of geopolitical centres such as will be summarized in the latter part of this chapter.

In today's scene, the notion of strategic location has not diminished in importance. Any exercise of influence still depends upon accessibility. Thus, the relative location with respect to power centres and transportation routes still vitally contributes to the identification of a strategic location. Geopolitical analysis must include the evaluation of the strength and spacing of centres of power and of the length, reliability and capacity of lines of transportation and communications.

CONNOTATION OF GEOPOLITICS

The power input into the geopolitical system may be expressed in terms of resources and economic potential. In this sense it may be construed largely as an expression of the human resources in all such ramifications as age, sex, education, employment, social structure and psychological characteristics, and also an expression of the availability of resources and the capability of resource development. Thus, major geopolitical power centres coincide with centres of population, production or commerce and they also form the focal points of the defence establishment. The importance of these power centres depends upon their inventory of advantages and upon how fast and how far influence can be projected from them. The general capability of a national economy to support a defence establishment is reflected in the estimated gross national product shown on the map in Figure 5. At this level of geopolitical analysis, military power should not necessarily be separated from economic or political power, for to an enemy all power centres carry the potential of objectives. All can loom as a threat, pinpointed by the enemy or only over his horizon in nebular perspective.

International Objectives : The central notion of geopolitics involves the concept that the relative strength of a state defines its ability to achieve international objectives. Within the same complex of thought, however, it can be implied that national power varies with accessibility from power centres. Therefore, the strength of a state determines the degree to which issues can be forced by diplomacy. In modern practice, international political strength is sought through the combination of states into alliances or international organizations which, in popular terms, may be called "power blocs". These take on some of the characteristics of a "suptastate".

The suprastate of today may take more than one form. It

may represent a definite grouping, though representing only a type of loose confederation, usually for special-purpose action, as SEATO or ANZUS. It may also represent an alliance composed of a dominant member and its allies as in the instance of the Warsaw Pact. Beyond these types, though not always deserving the label of suprastate, are the regional alliances and associations of former colonies. These make up international groupings in response to a recognition of common problems or a common cultural heritage. Examples include the Arab League, the Organization of American States and some eight or nine waxing and waning groupings among the 30 odd newly independent states of Africa.

GEOPOLITICAL FOCI

Geopolitics is truly a global science. In the world of today, states operate in continuous interaction one with another. Even continents and hemispheres cannot be isolated, strongly dependent on power centres on world location, movement, trade orientation and cultural or ideological bonds. In turn, the military prowess of states reflects these complexities, preventing any straightforward evaluation of powerhood by counting soldiers bearing arms, computing steel production indices or subjectively attempting to measure the will to fight as a human quotient. Prime motivations of international machinations as we presently know them stem from the complex of world sovereignties in force at any given moment. The national unit in its influence transcends all other political authority within the areal limitations of the state. It controls the administration of internal entities and dependent areas. At the same time, it remains the all important factor in any decisions on the operation of suprastates or direction of group action in regional affairs. Within its sovereign limits it can, for example, create, dissolve, or rearrange minor civil divisions and change the status of its dependent areas. And on an international scale, only the voices of national units other than in cases of force, elect whether or not or to what degree to participate in extranational groupings. As yet there is not and perhaps never can be, an international force endowed with the capabilities and authority to police the world or exert absolute power for the common good. One may conjecture that the Communist goal of world domination (or world liberation in the Communist sense) is a grotesque simulation to establish global order without danger of infraction.

So far as the rules sound simple, the nation state wields all-encompassing force in world affairs. But within the total framework of sovereignty exist some 125 independent states. From one to another they have only little semblance of uniformity in area, population, resources or in any other physical or cultural respect. The largest state (the Soviet Union) has more area than the 97 smallest states combined ; the most populous one (China) has more people than the sum total of the 96 least populated ones. Some have the resource potential sufficiently capable of developing and sustaining world power, others are virtually without resources beyond providing the means of bare subsistence for their inhabitants. Well over 100 dependent areas (mostly islands and groups of islands) further complicate the picture, concentrated as they are in the hands of 10 sovereign states. Another major element of extreme irregularity among sovereign states and productive of discord is the emergence since 1943 of 56 newly independent states into the world political arena. For the most part these latter are without the strongly held traditions, extensive political experiences or tested and proven administrative techniques commonly associated with viable states. Contrast the geopolitical concepts that one may associate with France and Germany as compared to those conjured up at the thought of Rwanda, Jamaica, Laos, or Western Samoa.

As recently as the early 1950s the world was dedicated to the situation of a bi-polarized world, consisting of two giant powers : the United States and the Soviet Union. The remainder of the world, either by choice or necessity, could do but little other than align its allegiances and sympathies with one or the other, or avow a policy of neutrality. The latter category tends to further divide into two alternates : (1) passive neutralism, whereby governments strive to avoid being drawn into the affairs of the colossi, and (2) aggressive neutralism, whereby governments make demands on or defy one or another or both of the strongest powers. At times the purpose of the latter national attitude is to draw concessions from either the Western or Communist worlds, or both, by "playing one side against the other", particularly well illustrated by political antics of certain of the newly independent states of Africa and Asia.

In the never-ending sequence of international events transpiring over a constantly changing world political pattern, one must now recognize a multi-polarized world. The United States and Soviet Russia have by no means relinquished their dominating roles in the world power structrue, but other states have in the last 10 years been steadily coming to the fore as secondary power centres. By a pooling of effort, combinations of these lesser but still significant sources of strength strive to further augment effective world positions. Statistics show, for example, that the accumulated power of the countries of Western Europe in theory, at least, would, if effectively combined, exceed many of the indices of strength held either by the United States or Soviet Russia. NATO, Benelux, the Common Market and Scandinavian Union all illustrate efforts at this type of amalgamation. The marshalling of strength by concerted effort among states, however, usually implies tremendous difficulties. Individual countries seem loath to sacrifice their national aspirations to a common cause notwithstanding potential and rather apparent advantages of cooperative effort. Suprastates at best have chinks in their armour, examples of which abound on every hand. Even the loose federation of a small number of states can be accomplished only by a long, slow process which must pass through one gruelling test after another. Arab states, for example, have failed in several attempts to combine other Arab states with them under a single flag or to effectively unify groupings politically ; such collective action cuts across the national interests of individual states and is a bitter pill to ambitious leaders of the weaker members of the group[1].

EGO-CENTRICITY OF NATIONAL POWER

National power over the surface of the globe follows no

pattern consistent with the distribution of sovereign states. Rather, it is ego-centric in design, dependent upon a wide range of attributes which permit and facilitate the development and maintenance of power on the part of any given state or ensemble of states. Dealing now only in broad fundamentals, the power structure involves the geographic, economic, demographic and resultant strategic elements offered by a particular centre. The strength amassed by such a power node gives primary impetus to foreign policy ; the greater the power, the greater the force to be exerted by the possessor. The ego-centric distribution of national power under consideration relies upon two basic concepts, both contingent upon the world location of the centre : (1) the resources and advantages at hand, and (2) the position with respect to all other centres.

The world can be scanned in identifying power centres, each one related to the multifarious factors which operate to create strengths or weaknesses. In the following paragraphs, 13 world regions are sketched to bring out highlights of power centres within them, or to ascertain area shortcomings and thus account for lack of power. The result should produce a notion of global power structure as applied to the deepening interrelationships in world affairs and as induced by a scaled-down time-distance factor.

STRATEGIC CENTRES

Anglo-America : Anglo-America constitutes the North American continent exclusive of its Latin segment in the southern part. Within it the United States, supplemented by a friendly Canada, has the attributes of a leading world power. Considerations of hemispheric defence make it desirable to include Greenland even though the island is a part of the Danish realm.

An abundance of resources, a concentration of population and a high level of economic development have combined to create major power nodes in the northeast quarter of the United States, including the general region of the Great Lakes and southeast Canada, particularly in the St. Lawrence Valley. Other less important but nonetheless significant power nodes skirt the Pacific Coast and the Gulf of Mexico. These areas of national strength reflect wealth and technological development, as a consequence making up focal points of maximum economic sophistication and highest standards of living.

From the standpoint of strategy, these highly developed power nodes are the major source of manpower and munitions for the nations in which they are located. To the degree that their functions may be pertinent, they comprise critical target areas in the event of attack. By their situation the requirements of hemisphere defence are to a degree defined. At the current level of technology, assault by air looms as the most likely threat and any counter measures centre about warning, interception and riposte. Warning systems are represented by the pine Tree Mid-Canada, and DEW radar lines or the patrols of surveillance along the continent. Interception is illustrated by the Nike installation and riposte by such widely divergent systems as Cape Kennedy. The Polaris submarines, or overseas bases. The optimum geographic distribution of the components of these defence systems depends upon the location of assumed prime targets, the estimate of the direction of attack, and an estimate of likely political alignments at the time of attack.

Cultural unity which affords common purposes of effort, further signals strength in the Anglo-American drive to a powerhood ensuring security in defence. Essential elements of the region include a similar history, similar political attitudes and a geographic coherence throughout the two large countries of which it is largely composed. English-speaking peoples dominate the region although Spanish-speaking and French-speaking minorities of consequence exist in southwestern United States and eastern Canada, respectively. Finally, aside from their common boundary, Canada has no other adjoining neighbours while the United States has no frontier problems more serious than a shifting Rio Grade separating it from Mexico.

Soviet Union : The Soviet Union incorporates a wide mixture of races and peoples which have been brought under the rule of a Slavic state by conquest. In this largest of all states a ruling minority dominates a nation of minorities. Here a vast assemblage of farmers, foresters and herdsmen has shown a remarkable ability in developing manufacturing and creating a relatively sophisticated economic structure. This development has been uneven, but appears to have first been built up as a power centre in the heart of European Russia and now is being extended in accelerated fashion to include central Siberia as far as Lake Baikal. As in Anglo-America, one can readily recognize power nodes within the Soviet Union, for example, Central Industrial Region, Donbas, Ural Region.

Transportation depends heavily upon railroads and inland waterways and to a much lesser degree upon highway traffic. It is seriously hampered during seasons of extreme cold or thaw. Thus, internal cohesion depends upon the people rather than upon accessibility.

This region holds the preponderant part of the "Heartland" of Sir Halford Mackinder[1] who postulated that its possession gave advantage for world conquest.[2] It is noteworthy that the heartland as originally conceived largely comprises a scantily populated, poorly accessible, inhospitable forest area. It seems quite possible that one could control such an area without the rest of the world ever hearing about it.

The essential element of Soviet geopolities lies in occupation of a central continental position, but primarily about the edges. The centre is hollow. Communications depend on approach through seasonally frozen waters. Interior land routes are poorly developed. Thus, the Soviet concern for outlets in the Baltic Sea, Turkish Straits, Indian Ocean and North China Sea has been reflected by Czarist and Communist governments alike. Now developments in air transportation and rocketry, however, have lessened dependence on surface communications and contacts.

Until the early 1950s, most Communist probes took place about the periphery of the country, as in Berlin, the Middle East and the Far East. More recently, however, trouble spots threatening world peace, many effected altogether or at least in part by the Soviet Union or its agents, have been erupting far beyond the zone of contact between the Communist and Western worlds, as in Cuba, Congo and Venezuela. These widespread symbols of world conflict by subversion illustrate the Russian determination to utilize to the maximum its geopolitical strength short of open conventional or nuclear hostilities by devices designed to upset the composure of Western diplomacy.

Western Europe: The eastern margin of Western Europe becomes difficult to determine. The exact line approximates the cleavage between the Western and Communist worlds until a few years ago popularly termed the "Iron Curtain." However, Albania and Yugoslavia present irregularities, the former a Communist enclave and the latter demanding a bracket apart because of its non-Soviet brand of Communism. West Berlin surrounded by East Germany also represents a disjunction within the peripheral zone, while Greece and Finland lie far to the east of where East Germany and Czechoslovakia thrust Communist territory to within 500 miles of Paris and London, further distorting any directional symmetry in the limits of the region. Within the 18 countries, however, making up the commonly accepted version of Western Europe, industrial and commercial activities have no equal elsewhere in the world in like concentration. Here are found the highest educational levels and greatest degree of sophistication in international politics. To trace the history of Western Europe is to trace that of the expansion of empires and of their collapse and fragmentation. The area served as a theatre for commercial and industrial revolutions, for the development of modern colonization and for the origin of proficient technical warfare.

Culturally, Western Europe has been crudely separable into two zones.[3] The northern area about the Baltic and North Seas is populated by people who speak a language related to Icelandic, hold to certain Germanic traditions of government and were leaders in the Protestant Reformation. The southern area fringing the Mediterranean has been historically dominated by ties to Rome. A Latin language, Roman Law and Roman Catholicism have tended to define cultural differences from the north, local applications of this pattern and transitional characteristics combine to create unique national patterns.

The principal centre of power in Western Europe corresponds to the North Sea Basin, with extensions to the east-northeast (as once exemplified by Hanseatic League activities), and to the east-southeast (as once exemplified by the push past Suez). Thus, the major power focus essential to play a dominating role in world polities within this heavily endowed region evidently cannot be controlled by a single state. Presently the direction of strength is turned toward a loose federation of most of the countries to comprise the heart of the North Atlantic Alliance. In addition, part of this subcontinental association seeks unity within itself by virtue of the European Common Market.

Individual countries of Western Europe, while prominent as power nodes within the region as a whole, have remarkable past records as geopolitical foci in their own right. Britain, France, Germany, Sweden, Spain, Portugal, Italy and Austria (though with different boundaries) have all within the last 500 years been first-class powers At present Britain and France, and to a lesser degree others of the 18 Western European countries, figure prominently among the world's 10 or 12 most powerful states.

Eastern Europe : Eastern Europe as defined here approximates those countries following the political system of the Soviet Union plus Communist Yugoslavia, itself formerly oriented towards the Soviet Union, Finland, geographically within the region, became independent from Soviet Russia in 1919 and has not actually been Communist-dominated since, despite its location and repeated dangerous overtures from Moscow. Should Europe be divided in such a way as to recognize a "central" region between west and east, the nomenclature presently used might have to give way to "Central Europe". However, the split between West and East by its bi-polar connotations has tended to give the continent two rather than three segments extending latitudinally.

Long inhabited by Slavonic and Fenno-Ugric peoples and largely of Roman Catholic faith, Eastern Europe may be closely associated with outside rule, whether Russian, Turkish, German or Austro-Hungarian. It has shown some attraction to the notion of Pan-Slavism. This unity was to a degree cemented by Russian conquest, the acceptance of Russian political systems and association in the Warsaw Pact. However, in recent years there have been signs that unity is deteriorating and that a spirit of independent action is growing. Hungary, Poland, Rumania and even Czechoslovakia have all given tangible evidence of active discontent with strong Soviet orientation.

The cultural development of Eastern Europe remains complex because foreign migrations, particularly by a ruling caste, have been evident. Cities differ strongly from the countryside and there are marked distinctions with the cities from one urban district to another as a result of complex cultural histories. A history of large landholdings first by nobles and later by the state as well as a history of mining and sophisticated manufacturing add to the unique pattern of scattered progress characterizing the region.

Because of this complex history, the region is torn among conflicting ethnic groups in which the conflicts spring from distinctions of language, religion, prestige and former status. Before World War II the region had earned for itself the term "shattered zone," a situation responsible for another geopolitical term "balkanization," to depict the fragmentation of empire.

Most of Eastern Europe has within the last two decades embraced a Communist political system. Nevertheless there is growing evidence of accessibility of the region to the West as illustrated by the heavy tourist traffic to the capital cities and resorts of the Black Sea Coast. U.S. aid to Poland and new trade agreements with Rumania are other examples. Yugoslavia, however, has over a longer period of time maintained open relations with countries of Western Europe and with the United States.

Single states within Eastern Europe can make little claim to national strength in themselves. Any sinews of war have since late 1940s been oriented towards Moscow, including the highly industrialized complex of Czechoslovakia. A reorientation of these states, either individually or collectively, suggests potential power within the region as traditionally implied by reference to the former military prowess of Central Europe, as in the case of Austria-Hungary during its more glamorous days.

Such a reorientation, however, has at the moment very little sustenance beyond idle conjecture.

Middle East : The Middle East, a region impossible to delineate precisely, usually refers to that cluster of states focusing on the tri-continental node of Asia, Africa and Europe. The greater part of the region lies in southwest Asia, extending as far north as the Soviet Union and as far east as Afghanistan and West Pakistan. In Africa, the United Arab Republic is always included and at times other large segments of the northern part of that continent as far as the Atlantic coast of Morocco. Turkey in Europe usually represents the stake of the third continent in the region, although in former times Bulgaria and Greece also looked towards Suez in formulating their political aspirations. Coastal configuration and land bridges involving the Mediterranean, Black, Aegean and Red Seas and the Persian Gulf have long given the Middle East a distinctive crossroads role. The desert-like landscape common to the preponderant part of the region plus enormous petroleum wealth in several of the political entities also help give it a unique geopolitical setting. In fact, the area centring around the shores of the Persian Gulf, contains 67 per cent of the world's proved petroleum resources and accounts for nearly 29 per cent (1963) of petroleum production. Kuwait alone yields nearly 2 million barrels of oil each day.

Culturally, the region finds unity based on the heritage of a common written language and strong religious traditions shared by the preponderant number of people. Countering these factors of unification, differences in the historical, economic and social aspects, while not overwhelming, have served to present the various political entities from existing in harmony and in seeking parallel goals. Pan-Arab congresses and the League of Arab States have proved more practical in theory than in actual practice.

The presence of Israel wedged among Arab states as well as some of Turkey's and Iran's cultural aspects which flank the Arab world gives to the region several striking diversities. Nevertheless the grouping of independent and semi-independent states making up the modern region also accounted for the nucleus of the great Ottoman Empire which in the sixteenth and seventeenth centuries thrust its power as far afield as the environs of Vienna.

Each of the major countries of the Middle East has proved itself capable of substantially influencing world power, illustrated by Turkey in its NATO role and the United Arab Republic in its political influence over wide blocs of territory. The latter country exerts a marked political influence over the new African states to the south and west and at the same time strives to champion any Pan-Arab movements. But standing alone—or even collectively—any integrated industrial base in the region which would support a major power centre is lacking. The role of the Middle East seems destined to be that of juxtaposition among other stronger powers, at times creating great tension either by political machinations from within the region or penetrating influences from without.

South Asia : The region now widely known as South Asia roughly corresponds to the concept of the Indian subcontinent. Division of the dominant country of the area into present-day India, Pakistan and Bangladesh together with existence of peripheral political entities—Afghanistan, Ceylon and the small Himalayan kingdoms of Nepal and Bhutan—has all but destroyed this image of a more or less continental bloc as well as reoriented the political outlook.

In a geopolitical sense, the region extends from the former British-Russian interaction zone of Moslem culture on the west to the former British-Chinese interaction zone of predominantly Hindi-Buddhist culture on the east.

Except for Afghanistan and the borderline cases of the Himalayan kingdoms, the entire area passed from European control to independent status immediately after the close of World War II. India and Pakistan were rent apart amid a bloodbath and still are divided by tensionridden boundaries, especially those associated with Kashmir and its cease-fire line. The Chinese attack of 1962 on India's northern periphery revealed a weak frontier zone capable of serious fracture. India's pacific attitude and continued attempts at neutrality towards a hostile China continue to pose problems to the West as well as to itself. Many of India's troubles also spring from within its own borders where conflicting forces based on contrasting regional and cultural interests have brought about political stagnation.

The relatively dry western part of South Asia comprises sparsely populated agricultural and pastoral land with a proud history but the scant economic development fails to support this national image. The eastern part, with a dense population and a trend towards industrial development, has a history of minority rule by Moslems or Christians, a restrictive social and economic structure and a limited level of educational and economic sophistication. Agriculture still predominates ; tribal societies still exist.

The enormous overall populations of the Indian Peninsula area have not in the past been converted into national strength of great consequence, nor does this likelihood seem plausible now. The cultural impact of language alone has had a remarkable effect, creating since independence many new internal state boundaries. Here regional interest won over those of the nation as a whole. Pressure on existing resources, lack of technical skill and paucity of capital for development invalidate the ample human resources. These handicaps, however, apply less to Pakistan than to India.

Southeast Asia : Southeast Asia is an assemblage of states which a long time ago were finely divided into independent and at times warring principalities. They have a history of enforced pacification and unification and of colonial rule by both European states and Japan. They comprise eight independent states including offshore Philippines and Indonesia and the two small dependencies of (British) Brunei and Portuguese Timor.[4] The region's Buddhist and Anamist cultural pattern has had Mohammedanism and Christianity introduced into it but with limited effect.

The six peninsular states of Southeast Asia—Burma, Cambodia, Laos, Malaysia, Thailand and Vietnam—dominate the economy of the area with plantations and commercial centres clustered about the coasts. Tribal societies persist in the interior and large segments of these countries do not participate in the national economy or politics.

Southeast Asia as a whole has been a zone of interaction with China for centuries ; Chinese colonization has intermittently taken place while parts have once been tributary to the Chinese Empire. Long ago there was an interaction between Hindu and Chinese cultures, followed by Moslem and Chinese culture, and more recently that between Europe and China. Since World War II American interests have focused upon the area, beyond former sovereignty ties and present friendly relations with the Philippines. The countries of Southeast Asia to a certain extent serve as a stress zone between the Communist and Free worlds with American military sponsorship involved in the concept of containment now in political favour, first evident in Laos and then in Vietnam.

Except for Thailand the eight countries are newly independent, seeking not only a national unity and personality but also the correct decision of how much of the culture and politics of China, India and the West they want to adopt for themselves.

The region as a whole represents a significant segment of Asia, comprising a world bloc highlighted in international intrigue. Its position as a transit zone on world routes from Europe to the Far East (as exemplified by Bangkok, Singapore, and Manila) with a bifurcation to the Antipodes, augments its global importance. Considerable amounts of physical resources in an area not overpopulated to the extent of nearby India and China, have long added to its attractiveness on the part of European states and currently on the part of China. Individual countries aspire to regional roles of prestige or leadership, as illustrated by Indonesia and Cambodia but a balanced industrial base in any one of them is insufficient for a sustained power drive. Even a theoretical grouping of these countries would find it difficult to build up and maintain a military power capable of carrying weight of global proportions.

Far East : The Far East consists essentially of the residue and fragments of the Chinese and Japanese empires except for those parts included in Southeast Asia and the Soviet Union. As a region it possesses only a vague unity of culture, history and national objectives. The level of economic and cultural development varies greatly within the region. Two power centres exist, one in Japan and the other in eastern China,

Two Koreas and two Chinas complicate the geopolitics of the Far East. Released from Japanese domination at the close of World War II, Korea failed to preserve independence ; the northern part of its territory fell into Communist hands under the guise of a people's republic. The island of Formosa inherited the exiled government of huge mainland China at the end of the 1940s when that area also fell under a Communist regime. More popularly known as Taiwan, the island now exists, with full support of the United States, as the legitimate seat of government of the Republic of China.

Currently and for many years past, the Far East has been a zone of interaction among the Russian, Western Europeans and Americans, into which both Chinese and Japanese have tried to interpose themselves as controlling elements. The conflicts of the Far East can be construed as a major encounter of competing European cultures with monolithic types of Mongolian and associated cultures.

Except for dry interior areas, the Far East is the most heavily populated region of the world, varied in cultures, languages and levels of economy and a region of limited resources. It is dominated by two contrasting regimes—Japan which has developed as a maritime nation and China, a power with a history of growth and interests mainly on land.

Japan, with the highest standard of living and greatest industrial knowhow in Asia, stands unique as a source of geopolitical strength in that continent. Unbridled human energy plus ready accessibility gave to the island empire hope to bid for a place in the sun—an effort well chronicled in the Pacific episodes of World War II. Now a challenge comes on the economic front, but testifying to a power complex of considerable potential.

Mainland China remains an enigma in the power structure of the Far East, indeed, of the world. With more people than any other country, evidence of both tapped and untapped resources and an aggressive Communist regime in control, the harsh statements coming out of Beijing may indeed sound fearsome. To counter this depressing vision of a giant on the loose, one can point to economic progress hardly matching the rising population, together with no effective military accomplishments other than infiltration beyond land boundaries by armed force to support outside allies and success in frontier-zone skirmishes.

Oceania : Oceania comprises Australia, New Zealand and those Pacific Islands not included in other regions, for example, New Guinea, Samoan Islands, Fijis and other groups in the Southwest Pacific. It consists of fragments of former British, German and Japanese colonial empires (including mandate or trust territories) and the residue of French and British colonies. In a geopolitical sense, the entire region lies remote from the conflicts of the rest of the world. Not many years ago the islands of the Southwest Pacific were important as bases and as "stepping stones" from North America to the Far East. Today technological advances have significantly diminished the importance of this function.

Until recent years Australia and New Zealand, commensurate with their earlier role in the British Commonwealth, furnished raw materials and products of minor labour effort to more heavily populated industrial countries in the Northern Hemisphere. Mounting industrial development, however, has given the countries "down under" greater viability and lessened their dependence upon long-distance inter-hemispheric trade. On a modified scale they have attained maturity in national strength, at least in relation to their remote location and with relative freedom from external conflict and without themselves being the scene of a conflict of cultures.

The future may see changes in relative locational situations because transportation improvements have brought these lands closer to Asia and the area of low population density may become increasingly attractive to those of the densely populated crescent of South and East Asia.

Northern Africa : Northern Africa is taken here to comprise the northern margin of the continent and southward into and through the power vacuum created by the broad Sahara desert. It encompasses old and well-established lands of Mediterranean Africa along with their dryland fringes to the south. The northern peripheries of a number of equatorial states also fall within the region, extending northward from another and vastly different area. Herein lies the incongruity of attempting to draw a geopolitical boundary or zone of contact, along an administrative frontier.

The northern part of the African continent has paradoxically been dominated by Moslem rule as well as by the colonial administration of European powers. The latter influence has denoted commercial penetration jealously guarded until recent years by outside interest. Local characteristics focus upon pastoral nomadism, grazing and grain culture. For the most part of the countries making up the region only recently received their independence. They have very sparse population, low levels of education, limited wealth and economic levels signifying underdevelopment. In the extreme north the people show most sophistication.

In a strategic sense, the states of Northern Africa[5] lack any efficient transportation system and have only a restricted capability to support any major military establishment. The region represents somewhat of an international power vacuum although its centuries of tradition, associated with ancient powers and position with respect to the Mediterranean, endow it with a prestige that has continuously attracted it to stronger states. During World War II, it provided the battleground par excellence for desert fighting, which in retrospect has proved classic.

Africa, South of the Sahara : The popular notion of Africa coincides with that part of the continent which lies south of the Sahara. Only here, over the broad savannas, in the equatorial region, on the eastern plateau and to the south, does the landscape adhere to these characteristics where colourful wild animals prowl over wild terrain with exotic vegetation. Moslem culture is strongest north of the tropical forest and along the east coast. However, south of the Sahara and in the Sudan, this influence becomes notably modified by local customs and the practices of Europeans.

The plateau of East Africa and the subtropical south have attracted European settlers far more than the hot humid lowlands of the broad equatorial band with the result that here are found the strongest white minorities, especially in the

Republic of South Africa. Geopolitical problems in Africa south of the Sahara tend to be in proportion to the percentage of white settlers in the area. In some instances, however, independence seems to have meant licence to resume tribal warfare as illustrated in Congo (Leopoldville). In the great surge of states becoming independent in this part of Africa, those without substantial white minorities commonly experienced the least difficulties in the transition from colonialism because of fewer points of tension. Thus, dependent entities such as Nigeria and Ivory Coast suffered less internal strife by minorities than did Kenya and Northern Rhodesia (now Zambia). Independence came with relative ease for the two former as compared with the two latter states where the interests of large numbers of white settlers were at stake in the face of new governments controlled by non-white elements.

In the equatorial part of the region and its periphery, the economy has been largely that of subsistence with a sprinkling of plantations of ranches. The lands are not only poorly developed and the new nations deficient in wealth but the assault on the cultural beliefs of the people has rendered them uncertain in coping with, to them, modern and fast-paced civilization. Here one finds not only an international power vacuum but a tinder box as well, illustrated by intermittent flare-ups of insurrection and Communist-inspired revolt.

In the extreme southern part of the continent, greater dominance of Europeans presents a different set of problems. More remote from the currents and conflicts of the rest of the world, these problems take on overtones quite independent of those common to major areas contiguous one to another. White colonization in South Africa, Southern Rhodesia and the Portuguese dependencies of Angola and Mozambique in some ways recall problems experienced elsewhere in the world decades earlier. Grazing, mining and other pioneer-like activities of this sub-region of secondary power focus are fraught with international tensions which differ from those in regions closer to the main arenas of international interplay. The Republic of South Africa, because of colour policies, has been even further isolated by resentment on the part of northern neighbours.

Central America : Middle America encompasses Mexico, Central America and the West Indian archipelago in the Caribbean. Caribbean margins of Colombia, Venezuela and possibly the three Guianas, in some instances, partake of the problems of the region and in other instances do not.

For the most part Middle America comprises Spanish-speaking countries with a history of Spanish colonial rule. A few French-speaking (Haiti, Martinique and Guadeloupe), English-speaking (Jamaica, Trinidad and Tobago and British Honduras), and Dutch-speaking (Curacao and Aruba) areas do exist though their combined extent represents less percentage than the region's total area. The population contains a strong assemblage of Indians, African Negroes and Europeans. The economy has until recently been dominated by plantation agriculture.

Only Mexico has an industrial potential which could qualify it as a strong regional power centre or secondary one in terms of world strength. Cuba's abortive attempt at industrial development under Castro and with Soviet tutelage gave evidence of geopolitical weakness in the island. The Panama Canal and plans for a second water route across Central America indicate transplantation of a major power function to a tributary geopolitical area.

The economy and cultural development of this region have been strongly influenced by the sea ; and traffic has been restricted and difficult. Thus, political cohesion remained difficult to attain and the vulnerability to sea-borne influences from seventeenth century pirates to twentieth century commercial enterprise, has left a strong imprint upon the region's culture, in part at least accounting for a high degree of heterogeneity. A broad history of coastal attack, overseas colonization, resources development by outsiders, revolution, territorial disputes and transfers and foreign intervention testify to these influences from without. Stability is currently being sought through education, economic aid and mutual political cooperation as illustrated by the efforts of the Alliance for Progress, the Organization of American States and private grants such as those sponsored by the Ford Foundation.

South America : For the most part South America has a history of Spanish or Portuguese colonization and of economic development based upon an assemblage of commercial plantations and ranches, subsistence agriculture, and extraction of raw materials. The proportion of Indians and Negroes to Europeans in the population varies inconsistently from place to place. Remoteness, inaccessibility, and isolation have been dominant elements in the political relations of South American states. Until the middle of the twentieth century, water transportation served to unite the peoples and most cultural development was close to water. These characteristics have long inhibited tendencies towards a unity of interest and action.

For over a century, South America has been a land of revolutions, local wars, dictatorships, and dependence upon foreign markets and manufactures. It suited the interests of some foreign states, particularly England and the United States to prevent additional foreign penetration and control in South America. In many respects South America was protected power vacuum. More recently, movements towards general education, agrarian reform, extended suffrage and economic diversification have appeared. As in the case of Middle America, the Alliance for Progress and other outside influences, such as financial assistance provided by the Inter-American Development Bank, are making inroads on the underdeveloped areas.

The continent has several power centres or nodes which would qualify as secondary, but stand incapable of generating great national strength. Only Brazil with its huge area, considerable population and ensemble of resources, offers a potential to rank as a world power, and only then under skilful statesmanship and industrial ingenuity. Elsewhere the national capitals plus a few mineral centres represent geopolitical foci which serve as mainsprings for the continent's rule in the world scene.

WATER SPHERES

Complementary to the 13 world regions and their associated power centres as above enumerated and summarily discussed are five peripherial spheres which support maritime action. Water area, too, holds strategic significance and is replete with geopolitical values. In themselves large water bodies do not constitute power centres *per se*, but rather play all-important roles in the spacing of land masses and islands that control the geopolitical strength of nations. Much has been written in geopolitical literature relative to the position of any state to the sea, ranging from those which are completely insular to the landlocked variety. In an overall sensing of unity the Pacific, Atlantic, Indian, Arctic Oceans and the Antarctic sphere of water and ice may coalesce to the single concept of a gigantic global sea.

Before the advent of air travel, the oceans of the world comprised the area of free movement and to a large degree defined the accessibility of nations. These areas, vast as they are, no longer have this unique position but remain of dominant importance in instances where massive, bulky or heavy traffic is essential. For these reasons it is the margins of oceans in low and middle latitudes, particularly in restricted waters intricate with embayments and narrow passages, that figure most prominently in international power politics.

REFERENCES

1. Groupings of political entities in this list, arranged in combinations, have certain geographic and political characteristics in common. It may be noted that these regions correspond in most instances to blocked-out areas featured in the news of the day : Anglo-America, Soviet Union, Western Europe, Eastern Europe, Middle East, South Asia, Southeast Asia, Far East, Oceania, North Africa, Africa South of the Sahara, Middle America and South America.
2. Mackinder first presented his notion of a heartland in 1904 (Mackinder, H.F. : "The Geographical pivot of History, "*Geographical Journal*, 23 (1804). At this time he gave emphasis to the coherence of an area of potential internal, overland communications which gave a high degree of flexibility in direction of land movement. Such a pivotal area was his heartland. He varied his notion in later years. In 1943 (Mackinder, H.F. : "The Round World and the Winning of the Peace, "*Foreign Affairs*, 21, No. 4 (July 1943), she presented the

heartland as shifted in location so as to eliminate some sparsely populated mountain and forest areas. Most recently Mackinder appears to have imagined the heartland as a "citadel of power" based on population, resources and transportation.

3. Iceland, Ireland, the United Kingdom, Norway, Sweden, Denmark, Finland, the Netherlands, Belgium, Luxembourg, France, Spain, Portugal, Italy, Switzerland, the Republic of Germany, Austria and Greece, but excluding the microstates (Andorra, Monaco, etc.), European Turkey and arbitrarily eliminating Malta on the basis of its short-lived sovereignty and Yugoslavia for political and cultural dissimilarities.
4. The Six peninsular states of Southeast Asia : Burma, Cambodia, Laos, Malaysia, Thailand and Vietnam.
5. The term North Africa, as distinguished from northern Africa, frequently refers only to Morocco, Algeria and Tunisia. Northern Africa is roughly synonymous to the Maghreb, Arabic term referring to the northern segment of Africa.

CHAPTER THREE

GEOGRAPHY AND WAR STRATEGY

Both geography and strategy are imprecise words with elastic meanings. They may be concerned with the world at large, the land and water masses, the globe itseif with all its resources. They may be concerned with narrower but no less important considerations : the characteristic of a coast, a country, a province, a mountain chain or a river valley.

Today more than ever the strategist, like the economist, has to look upon the world as a whole. I do not mean by this that distance has been abolished, that is a cant phrase which may lead to absurdities. It would be absurd, for instance, to say that modern weapons and means of communication have made New Zealand as vulnerable as the British Isles. Common sense tells us that it is not. But the modern conqueror who succeeds in dominating the main land masses of the world, will have everything else speedily added unto him. New Zealand will not long elude his clutches. Strategically as well as geographically, the earth is a whole. And the earth is something about which we know surprising little. Even its precise shape is not quite clear and it seems to be subject to changes in shape of which we know nothing. We make maps, that is projections on paper which are of course conventional and the projection which the public know best is the most unimformative and even deceptive of course Mercator's. We compile lists of the times and levels of tides ; but they go out of date without our noticing it. Only a very small proportion of the earth have we covered by instrumental survey, and wonderful as modern methods of photographic surveys are, they have not yet replaced instrumental survey on the ground.

The more we study the world, the more we feel the gaps in our knowledge of it. Professor Taylor suggests that the exact size and shape of the earth may by elevated to the rank of "top secret" and that for a country to be ill-mapped might provide a species of camouflage. Both may well be the case.

And if it be objected that the modern system of stereoscopic survey from the air, though not the equal of ground triangulation with astronomical observation, will still render it possible for every part of the globe to be relatively well mapped, infinitely better than it has ever been before, but this is nevertheless the sort of intelligence which it may be difficult to obtain, especially in time of peace. And even in war it would be hard for photographic aircraft to penetrate deeply into a territory of vast extent so as to cover more than a fraction on the outskirts. Here the little country may be handicapped in comparison with the big one because a little country may be much more easily photographed against its will. And here also the democratic nation may be handicapped as against the totalitarian because a democratic nation does not conceal its geographical surveys. Yet even in democratic countries, certain features being omitted from the maps of the future.

Military geography should be a subject of study for the commander and staff officer. They can get from it not only concrete information but also general ideas which may be of high value to them in their profession. The features of a country, its mineral and agricultural wealth, its situation with regard to world communications and their junctions, do in fact go far towards determining that country's destiny.

The qualification of a great power today depends largely upon its minerals, above all coal, iron ore and oil, though many others may be added, some of which have a special application to its actual armaments for war. But it must also possess the basis for a great and vigorous population, and this implies big stretches of lowland, reasonable well watered, with soils suited to certain grain crops and to cattle. Political and social conditions, situation with regard to the most advanced forms of civilization, may retard its rise to power as they did to a striking extent in the case of Russia and even more so in the case of Japan previously. But if it has the qualifications, it will sooner or later enter into the ranks of the great nations ; and then its rise may be very rapid. As world time is measured, it was rapid in the case of Russia and astounding in the case of Japan. A nation need not be altogether self-sufficing, but if not it must possess natural communications with outside sources of wealth or secure them for itself by sea power. One can think of various other attributes of power. Falling water is one of the chief of them, and this is an age of great power dams. A moderate and equable climate is another, but not a necessity. Russia has an extreme climate which condemns its agricultural population to long spells of inactivity, yet this has not prevented the developement of great agricultural wealth. But to a certain extent climate and race are linked. It seems to be the mixed climates which produce the highest human energy, even when they go to extremes.

Not long ago the American airman, General Spaatz, pointed out that the qualifications of great powers today were to be found only in the northern hemisphere. They were to be found above all in his own North American continent, in Northern and Central Europe and perhaps in a block of territory comprising India, Japan, Korea, Manchuria and adjacent parts of China and Far Eastern Russia, all in the northern hemisphere. The northern hemisphere is a land hemisphere, the southern a water hemisphere. Apart from these European and Asiatic blocks, nowhere else in the world were there regions which could constitute a peril to the United States within measurable time. This factor, he said, must greatly modify United States' military policy in an age of long-range weapons. And he pointed out an entirely new feature in the strategic situation of North America, the fact that the northern fringes of Europe and Asia, from North Cape in Norway to East Cape on the Bering Strait, formed a rough semi-circle of the Old World facing another semi-circle of the New World formed by the North coast of Greenland, the arctic islands norths of Canada and Alaska; while Alaska itself, looking westward, almost touched Far Eastern Russia. He thought it possible that some long-range weapons might be projected across the polar region into the North American continent. But these intensely cold areas had no strategic significance whatever in the past-accounts for the fact that Canada and the United States now look north as well as in other directions, and accounts for the defence measures taken in concert by the two states to cover approaches from this hitherto disregarded direction.

What General Spaatz said about the impossibility of a great world power appearing within measurable time anywhere outside the northern hemisphere was perfectly true ; but there are land masses in the southern hemisphere, small by comparison with those of the northern but in many respects richly dowered and capable of exerting great strategic influence and perhaps of swinging over the balance of power one way or the other, according to the direction in which they lean. One is Australia with New Zealand and the East India Islands, the last lying mainly south of the equator. Here we have the only white population in the Pacific and immense wealth of raw materials. Australia and neighbouring territories have not the full qualifications of a world power for as far ahead as we can see, but they are potentially a power of the second order and may exert great strategic influence.

The second is of course South America, prosperous, still expanding, one of the world's great food depots as well as rich in other respects. South America is mainly in the southern hemisphere, the equator running north of the Amazon. And this continent lies much closer than does the United States itself to the Panama Canal which is of such vital importance to the U.S. strategy. There we see in the recent Treaty of Raio, fathered by the United States but not imposed, that it is possible in these days of what are called power politics for the greatest power in the world to gain legitimate ends without threats or bullying.

And then there is Africa, for though only about a quarter, anywhere less than one-third of African territory lies in the southern hemisphere, this fraction contains a larger proportion of its actual and potential wealth. South of the equator there are to be found huge resources virtually untapped until this generation and capable of being almost indefinitely expanded. And they are, so to speak, tucked away behind the immense barrier of the Sahara. Africa might become a storehouse from which the present shortages of Europe could be largely supplied.

In Africa too there is an alliance between economic and strategic possibilities. Its northern shore fringes the Mediterranean, its eastern, the Red Sea and the Arabian Sea, great traffic routes of the world. And to put matters in a concrete form, the continent flanks a possible Russian drive across Western Europe and may thus be considered as a base for counter-offensive. It is not possible to imagine Africa as great power in itself, at all events not in this country nor perhaps in the next, but in a very much shorter space of time, it might become a great adjunct of power.

In military books a quotation from Archduke Charles says that "the Danube is the strategic key to southern Germany and that the result of wars there is always decided upon the Danube." These words may cause vagueness about what the writer means. But the implication here is that there is a long stretch of the Danube, from Ulm to Regensburg, where there were in his day—and the general conditions have not enormously changed—a dozen good crossing-places with bridges. Farther downstream, from the Isar to the Inn, there was only a single crossing, that at Passau, and no road along the left bank. But from Ulm to Regensburg there were these twelve crossing-places and excellent communications.

The geographical study of a theatre of war I want to make is that of the Burmese theatre of war. I need not remind you that the campaigns in Burma were fought in the most disadvantageous way. A first look at a geographical map shows us that the natural way in which to fight a campaign in Burma from a base or bases in India is through Rangoon and, therefore, that the natural way in which to open it would have been to retake Rangoon first of all. It is all very well to say that the Indian Government in the years before the war ought to have improved the land communications with Burma. But I feel sure that if you had to pick the objects on which to spend a limited amount of money, you should have put a road or roads from India into Burma on a relatively low priority. After all England was a naval nation, not what Mr. Churchill calls a "land animal." If England lost command of the sea, all calculations would be upset. To envisage inability to maintain sea routes between Calcutta or Colombo and Rangoon, they had to presuppose not only a simultaneous war with Germany or Japan but also the complete overthrow of France; for it was that which brought the Japanese into French Indo-China and Siam. They had to presuppose a disaster such as the sinking of the Price of Wales and the repulse without their having inflicted damage on the Japanese fleet. They had to go even further and presuppose such calls from the European theatre of war that they should not to able to allot coastwise craft to Burma even when there was a possibility of using them. As early as the winter of 1942-43, there was a possibility of using such craft to secure Akyab but at the last moment Field Marshal Wavell was informed that they were not available, being required for the landings in the Mediterranean theatre. So the capture of Akyab was attempted by an advance down the Arakan, which failed after heavy fighting.

Not until the very end was the naval material for the coming in sufficient strength for the capture of Rangoon by sea, though a little was produced earlier on the Arakam coast. And when it was produced to take Rangoon, it arrived too late for practical purposes. They did land at Rangoon, but to find it empty. General Slim had by this time already won the campaign on overland communications and air supply and transportation, and it may be said the Rangoon landing can be said to have made any great difference in the long run.

And so the campaign of General Slim and of the American-directed Chinese forces which started from the Hukawang valley had to be conducted in the most difficult of all ways. There were no roads leading from Assam across the huge jungle-clad ridges which barred the way to the valleys of the Chindwin and the Irrawady. Everything had to be improvised. But none of the extraordinary work accomplished, such as that of the American railway battalions on the Bengal-Assam railway, would have sufficed to provide a basis for a successful compaign entirely over land communications. It could not have been done. To atone for the weaknesses of the land communications, inventive minds set themselves to work out revolutionary methods of air transport. These were produced under the pressure of sheer necessity.

The tactics of the campaign were influenced as well as the strategy. Thus, a division marching along a valley would not necessarily have to seal it off behind as in normal circumstances. The divisional commander did not have to waste troops by stringing them out along his line of march. So long as he had a strong rearguard, it did not matter much to him if the Japanese flowed into the valley in his wake. And this new conception of administration, which may have so important an effect upon warfare of the future, was created by the terrain itself, by these gigantic off shoots of the Himalayas which are called the Lushai hills, the Naga hills, the Patkai hills, and farther south the Arakan Yoma and Pegu Yoma which overhang the basin of the Irrawady ; and created also by the difficulties of operating in the natural way over sea communications.

In Europe the Rhine can be outflanked in Holland, but the nation which has always up to the present century, and to some extent in the present century, desired to force a passage of the Rhine from west to east has been France, and France could only turn the Rhine barrier if she possessed control over Holland, which was not often. When Britishers went into Holland, it was not generally for the purpose of forcing the Rhine barrier but in order to keep the French out of the Low countries. On the two occasions in this country when England fought as allies of the French, they were unable to gain possession of north Holland and so could not outflank the Rhine barrier. The country is in any case not very suitable for operations because it is so easily inundated by a defender. In World War I Holland's neutrality was respected; so the question never arose. In World War II, Holland's neutrality having been earlier violated by Germany, it did arise. As the

21st Army Group's spearhead was thrust northward into Holland, there seemed every chance that the task of outflanking the Rhine barrier might this time be accomplished. If it had been, it would have had a very important effectup on the future of the campaign because there are no obstacles of any importance, except those of the soil itself, in passing round the elbow of the Rhine until the Ems is reached; the Ijjsel cannot be called a serious barrier.

But there were three factors which fought against England. The number of water obstacles was the first. The Rhine divides into two channels, the southern called the Waal, the northern the Lok or, higher up opposite Arnhem, the Nodor Rhin. Farther south the Mass or Mouse for a short distance follows a parallel course forming another great water obstacle. And as if nature had not done enough to make things difficult, man has thrown in two parallel canals, the first known as Mouse-Escaut or Mass-Scheldt, the second the Albert canal. The second factor was the nature of the soil, particularly north of the Mass where it is spongy even for Holland. The third was the bad weather, especially disadvantageous when allied with this sponginess of the soil, which practically confined the advancing column to the main road. The bad weather did not come as a complete surprise to them because rain in September is common enough in Holland. And so, despite the skill in mounting a triple airborne operation and the gallantry with which it was carried out, especially at Arnhem, the 21st Army Group leapt four barriers, the two canals, the Mass and the the Waal, but failed to maintain its footing beyond the last. This failure modified not only the Group's strategy but the whole of the Allied strategy in the west until the passage of the Rhine had been effected. Everybody knows something of the story of Arnhem but there must be a great number of people who fail to grasp the significance of the episode because they do not connect first of all the motive involved, the turning of the line of the Rhine, and secondly its fate, with the nature of the country, in fact, with the local geography.

I will end with a story told to Mr. Cyril Falls of Oxford University, by General Laycock in 1944, soon after the Allied landing in lower Normandy. At an early stage in the planning, he put three small teams which were not to communicate with each other until they had their results ready, on to the problem of deciding where the landing ought to be made. They all produced the same answer—the bay of the Seine. That appeared to him not only striking but actually perturbing. By this time he knew that the Planning Staff had actually plumped for the bay of the Seine though his teams did not know it and he thought that if there was such extraordinary unanimity on the subject on our side, the German intelligence would certainly have come to the same conclusion. If fact, it does not seem to have done so.

The point I want to make is that to the mind which has been specially trained to work along such lines geography will constantly hold out a key to strategic problems. But it requires intense application and a most diligent accumulation of facts before the problem can be answered with certainty and unanimity. Obviously you will never get either all that application or all that information in time of peace. But we can in time of peace train the minds and the eyes of the men so that if ever they are called to work on unknown paths, the way will be familiar to them.

CHAPTER FOUR

GLOBAL GEO-STRATEGY

OLD CONCEPT

In a land-or sea-based concept of military strategy, the earth's surface, features and conditions play an inevitable part and operations of any kind must take them into account. Of the two, land power is most closely linked to geo-strategy, since the movement by land and the use of land forces is vitally concerned with the conditions of the terrain, its mountains, plateaus, and plains and with weather conditions that may hamper troop transport or tactical movements. Hannibal's crossing of the Alps, the Battle of the Bulge, or the defeat of Napoleon at Waterloo—these were military actions and movements *on land*, in mountains, on a dissected plateau and on a plain. They were struggles for the control of a land space of no great size in itself, and their outcome depended on superior weapons, land transport, military strategy and large numbers of combatants. In such conflicts the conditions of the local topography play a large part in attaining success in warfare. Certainly no commanding officer could risk inadequate knowledge of the geographic and geo-strategic setting in which the immediate conflict was to take place. To do so might well predetermine the military outcome. On the contrary, well-trained army personnel are well informed by aerial survey, maps, models, briefing and other devices concerning the terrain problems they must face. By way of contrast, the airman is freed from the need for detailed knowledgc of such extent ; his briefing takes a different form but it is no less important.

Naval activities in wartime are closely tied to the geo-strategy of the sea areas and their coasts, involving restrictions of movement imposed on them by straits, channels, shallows, capes, reefs and the like. Though perhaps less circumscribed by geographical conditions than a land army, military strategy at sea cannot be completely free from the influence of winds, adverse weather and ocean currents. While there may be some changes in the more critical spots, such as the construction of a Suez Canal to enable the western fleet to shorten the time required for its contacts with the Orient, the seaman nonetheless is not free to pursue any route he may wish, and the very nature of his method of transportation necessarily inhibits his activities and governs his military strategy and policy. His primary concern is with the open sea or the coasts ; large land masses as such have little or no bearing upon his thinking except as they may impede the freedom of his movements around the globe. The addition of an air arm, however, increases the area that may be placed under the control of naval units although, since naval aircraft normally is regarded as secondary to the fleet itself, they are not at liberty to take full advantage of the freedom of action and world-wide operations that full use of the air afford.

In the following discussion in this chapter, the long-established and recognized basic elements that have been regarded as significant in any presentation of political or military geo-strategy have been presented briefly ; these are (1) size, extent or expanse of a political unit, (2) the importance of location on the earth's surface, (3) strategic position with reference to other geographic and political units, (4) the focal points of land and sea transport, (5) political boundaries zones, and (6) buffer states. Later, an evaluation of these and other geographic factors in the light of the needs of military aviation will be presented.

SIZE AND SHAPE

There was a time when a nation of great size could consider itself reasonably secure from attack by hostile neighbours, if attacked, could withdraw some distance within its borders, thus falling back on a land area that provided a hard core of resources with which to fight back. Not only was its size a factor, but in this concept of strategy, time is the well-known "defence-in-depth" idea, successfully tried on many occasions and long regarded as one of the most important military advantages of a nation as large as India and the United States. It was believed particularly effective when the nation in question also enjoyed sea boundaries.

There is no "ideal" size for a nation. Its extent of land should be sufficient to allow its people to produce most of the food they consume without undue overcrowding and lowering of living standards. The situation should be refined even more : a nation should have sufficient land area that is *productive.* West Africa occupies an area larger than a million square miles, but by far the larger part of that land is unsuited for agriculture and remains relatively unpopulated because its moisture deficiency is so great that it will support only small numbers of people in relation to its size. In comparison, Great Britain, with an area less than 100,000 square miles, supports three times as many people as West Africa.

"Size alone is not strength, only potential strength. Arable areas, manpower, industrial organization, raw material resources are pre-requisites of power whether on land or on sea (or in the air). Yet the larger area gives greater chance for climatic range and varying topography and, therefore, varying resources and economic possibilities......The facts of topography condition internal control quite apart from the danger of aggression from without, because only with effective centralized control does large size become an element of strength rather than a weakness. This control in turn depends on communications and configuration Obviously, shape is important—a compact circular area being preferable to a drawnout shoestring—yet topography is more significant in determining the ease of communication within a country which will vary greatly with the height or form of mountain ranges, the depth and width of valleys, the direction of rivers, the location of marshes or of deserts and the modifying effect of climate on all of these."

The area of a nation, then, must be considered carefully by those in charge of any military operations and planning. As the quotation suggests, large size is desirable up to an undetermined point ; beyond that, the problems of transport and communication become so great that the nation tends to fall apart rather than act as an organized unit. Hitler found, in penetrating Russia's "defence in depth," that the great distances from his base of operations in Germany militated against the success of his invasion. His defeat at Stalingrad was certainly due in large part to the difficult problems of transport of goods and men over the vast expanse of the Russian steppe lands.

If the transport system within a nation is inadequate to meet the needs or is poorly developed, great land areas may lead to the development of a marked internal disunity, but not all improvements in communication and transportation necessarily result in greater national unity. The expanse of Siberia was too much for the thin thread of the Trans-Siberian Railway to unify after the completion of the line in 1906. It did have a bearing, however, on Russia's stronger hold on the provinces of eastern Asia.

LOCATION

Except for a few outlying places, the most important part of the world from the economic, political and military standpoint for many centuries has been located in the lower middle latitudes and the mid-latitudes of the northern hemisphere. The distribution of land masses on the face of the earth has been the primary reason for this localization of power aided by climatic conditions prevailing in this part of the world. The repressive environments of the low and high latitudes and to some extent the high altitudes have prevented the development of civilizations that would support important political units.

Thousands of years ago the milder environment of a subtropical land and the less well-developed stages of civilization provided the ideal setting for the growth of strong states, as in Egypt, India southern China, or Iraq. At a later time in history the emphasis shifted away from low latitudes in the direction of Rome, and then to the Iberian peninsula and Spain and Portugal. Modern times have witnessed the development of great military and economic strength in mid-latitude locations such as Germany, France, the Netherlands, England, the Soviet Union and the United States. The factor of location on the face of the earth, therefore, was a paramount consideration in any view of history.

If, in addition to a favourable mid-latitude location and wide expanses of territory, a particular state is so situated that it is in a position to dominate or command the movement of people and goods of all kinds by land and sea, then its strength may be materially enhanced since it can engage in profitable trade and commerce and serve as a focus of major transportation routes. During the Renaissance the city-state of Venice at the head of the Adriatic Sea occupied a strategic geographic position. On the sea it developed a strong naval force and merchant marine. On land, certain commercial trade routes crossing the Alps converged on Venice and the command of an important pass from the Adriatic to Vienna tapped the hinterland of that city. Food supplies from the fertile plains of the Po river were at hand, and Venice, with these advantages of strategic position, dominated trade routes between north western Europe and the Orient. The wealth acquired in this manner as well as other advantages, maintained sufficient military strength to protect her commercial empire for a long time.

It does not necessarily follow that strategic position of great importance may lead to development of a strong state. Unquestionably the Isthmus of Panama was strategically important long before the construction of the Panama Canal in 1914, but no strong power controlled or commanded the Isthmus until after the construction of the canal, a matter which greatly enhanced the strategic character of the Isthmus. Even today, the nation most directly concerned with the land area of the Isthmus—the Republic of Panama, is a weak military state. The land contiguous to the Canal itself, the Canal Zone, is controlled by the United States, a power far stronger than that represented by the Republic of Panama. Somewhat parallel conditions prevailed at the sthmus of Suez prior to the construction of the Suez Canal in 1869.

FOCAL POINTS AND CONDITIONS OF LAND TRANSPORT

Wherever there is interference with normal land routes, interruption of travel often leads to the pinpointing of a critical spot that acquires national and international importance. Upon occasion these localities are the subject of disputes that lead to armed warfare ; they may be strongly fortified. Their control in former years often decided whether a nation was able to defend itself or whether it was able to dominate important roads or other routes in order to add to its wealth and power. Large water bodies, swift streams or extensive swamplands may provide natural barriers to land transportation, difficult to overcome when large number of troops or quantities of war material must be moved by highway or rail.

Large water bodies, particularly lakes and bays, are not impossible to cross but they may retard land movement and may occasionally be impassable during an armed conquest. This was true in 1940 when the Germans all but succeeded in crossing Dover Strait to invade the British Isles. In June, 1944, when the Allied armies used England as a spring-board for the Normandy invasion, the crossing of this same narrow body of water was a difficult and expensive accomplishment. In general, obstructions caused by rivers are not as serious, and while the necessity for crossing a stream may slow down the rate of movement of troops, it is generally possible to do so without too much difficulty or interference, assuming that actual attack does not occur while the crossing is in progress, or that the crossing is not under aerial attack. In 1971 the Indian army presented a remarkable river crossing operation in East Pakistan and liberated Bangladesh in a shortest possible time, recorded in the history of modern warfare.

Of greater consequence are large areas of highly mountainous land in certain parts of the world. These are difficult to traverse on foot or in vehicles, and for centuries of human history they have prevented easy transport and communication between peoples living on opposite sides of such mountain zones. Evidence of this interference appears on present-day maps in the form of occasional political boundaries that coincide with mountain crests ; among others, the summit of the Andes, the Pyrences, parts of the Alps, the Himalayas and the Caucasus. Focal points of great importance in mountain areas are most likely to develop at altitudes lower than the crests in mountain passes. In the past, important military movements or engagements have taken place in strategic spots like Kasserine Pass, the Mohawk River corridor, the Vienna gateway on the Danube, Khyber Pass, or the Moravia Vardar valley in the Balkans.

Land travel may be interrupted by seasonal weather conditions. A river, for example, might pose no problem to transportation during most of the year, but in flood season such a stream would be impassable for an armed force for several weeks at a time. Normal crossing places such as fords might be useless during the flood season. Another seasonal interruption to land travel may result from excessive rainfall ; this is important in those parts of the world having dense populations and large urban centres. A protracted season of snow and cold has hampered active military operations on land as it did during the excessively severe winter in which Washington and his troops were snowbound at valley Forge. In more recent years, winter weather conditions played a large part in the attack or the Germans during the battle of the Bulge.

LIMITATIONS OF TRANSPORT BY SEA

Obstacles of sea transport may be as difficult to surmount as those by land. The seaman may have to contend with inhospitable or dangerous shores like the coast or Oregon which has unsatisfactory anchorage or poor harbour conditions; excessive tidal range like that at Liverpool ; or total lack of shelter when his vessel is at anchor. To some extent, these problems can be overcome by proper engineering of port works, dredging of channels, or the erection of lighthouses or coast guard stations.

The seaman must take into account the conformation of those land areas bordering his seas. This is particularly important if some major obstruction lies athwart his chosen route. It might be a large island, a dangerous ice field or icebergs, a sand bar or a shoal. The sailor must be thoroughly familiar with these factors of marine geography and many others as well. Though such obstructions may not completely impede his progress, they do mean that he must take a longer route to reach his destination, or that arrival at that point will be delayed. Narrow water bodies may be too constricted to allow safe passage ; tempting as the presence of a narrow strait may be, it can become a trap for the careless navigator. To select a specific example, it is regarded as unwise to allow even small or medium-sized vessels of the United States Navy to take passage through the Strait of Messina since its width is too narrow and the strait is too shallow to assure reasonable safety. In addition, strong currents make the strait a hazardous passage at times.

BOUNDARIES

In the past, political and military geo-strategy has been greatly concerned with international boundaries, and appropriately so in view of the numerous cases in which a boundary dispute has led to war between neighbouring nations. Certainly the airman should be familiar with the locations and character of international boundaries and the problems arising from them, but for air travel they pose no physical barriers and in those parts of the world where national areas are limited in extent as in western Europe, it is easy to become confused concerning boundary locations. To cite an example of such confusion,

"Berne, Switzerland, April 1, 1944. At least 50 persons were killed and more than 150 seriously wounded when 30 American four-motored bombers in three waves swooped out of a cloud formation at 15,000 feet just before 11 o'clock this morning and rained explosives and phosphorus incendiary bombs on the northeastern Swiss town of Schaffhausen. Their probable objective was the German town of Singen, about 11 miles north of Schaffhausen and an important railroad junction on the German-Italian railroad lines."

"The commander of one of the groups of Liberator bombers said that "We are terribly sorry that it happened". We were simply blown off our course by a wind of higher velocity than anticipated."

"At least six factories were completely wiped out by the explosions in Schaffhausen, while extensive damage and loss of life occurred when a cluster of bombs dropped on the corner of a market place where the weekly session was in full swing."[2]

Even when two bordering nations are not at war, the flier must still be aware of the presence of their international boundaries. Before 1940, for example, aviators in Finland were ordered to remain a stated distance from the Russian boundary since international tension was mounting at that time and the Republic of Finland was anxious to avoid any unfortunate incident that might provide Russian authorities with a pretext for undertaking reprisals.

Today, the boundary of greatest critical importance is the Russian territory, separating the Communist-controlled nations of Europe from those of the non-Communist world. Its presence is a source of great political, social and economic friction, and even though it represents a land boundary, its significance must be appreciated by, and its location known to, every European. Of shorter length, the boundary separation of Communist Korea from the Republic of Korea represents a similar situation on the Asiatic continent.

Most international boundaries of the world are reasonably stable for long periods of time but certain special locations have been recent trouble spots, giving rise to demonstrations of nationalism, occasional rioting and demands for military action. At times it has been possible to settle these arguments by mediation but where this is not a satisfactory solution, the disputed boundary may become a matter of such profound importance to the people of the nations involved. The extensive land fortifications, plainly-marked boundary lines, boundary patrols or other schemes are put into operation in order to keep the dispute from breaking into open warfare.

Some international boundaries seem to be justified in their location but marked coincidence with the natural aspects of geography. Usual examples include the Andean mountain boundary between Chile and Argentina, the Pyrenses between France and Spain, the northern boundary of India along the Himalayas, and other similar localities. These natural features may take the form of mountain ranges, as above, or they may be narrow seas, rivers or other features. As a rule the international boundary that is well marked by mountains tends to be reasonably stable and this is also true of boundaries that traverse lakes. There has been no recent challenge by either party to the international boundary along the Great Lakes and the St. Lawrence River between Canada and the United States. Rivers on the other hand make very poor international boundaries. They may be crossed with relative ease and since the river channel may change position occasionally, question then arises concerning the changing position of the boundary line.

In the absence of natural features in some parts of the world, there has been a tendency to locate international boundaries with reference to compass directions, parellels and meridians. The Canadian-American boundary from Lake-of-the Woods westward is a surveyed boundary bearing no reference whatever to natural features until it reaches the Strait of Juan de Fuca, where it takes account of the water barrier separating Vancouver Island from the mainland. Even there, a dispute arose over the placing of the boundary among the San Juan Islands but the problem was finally worked out to the satisfaction of both nations after necessary mediation.

Many political units in Africa are plotted with surveyed boundary lines having no reference to natural features of importance. This is often the case where it is believed the land is of little value and resources are seemingly lacking, as in the interior parts of Libya, West Africa and elsewhere. The subdivisions of Australia are planned in much the same way, and in general, this practice applies in those parts of the world that have experienced comparatively recent settlement.

It is evident that any one of these different types of boundaries could become a matter of argument, and if sufficiently bitter, the dispute could in turn lead to international warfare on a major scale. It is therefore necessary to be aware of the dangers inherent in violated international boundaries and that they be as full informed as possible concerning the causes of potentially unstable boundary zones. These are the places that should be watched if armed aggression resulting from boundary disputes is to be avoided in the future.

BUFFER STATES

As long as military activities are concerned primarily with movements by land, certain political devices can be used to provide some degree of protection against invasion by a hostile power. One of these, the traditional "buffer state" has been used many times to provide a neutral zone between two powerful nations whose borders would otherwise be contiguous. The buffer state is nothing more than a line. Obviously such a state must be weaker in a military sense than either of those nations that it separates if it is to serve its proper function as a boundary zone between them.

There have been many examples of the use of buffer states in the past. Among these during the last half century we may include Poland, separating Germany and the Soviet Union ; Belgium and Holland, separating parts of France and Germany; Austria, Czechoslovakia and others. At times the buffer state is a political unit set up without reference to the language, culture, economies or wishes of its own citizens. It may, indeed, encompass a wide variety of cultures, as in Czechoslovakia or it may be based upon a relatively homogeneous people like the Dutch of the Netherlands.

Though this type of political unit may on occasion accomplish the purpose for which it was established, conditions of modern warfare and the development of rapid transport have neutralized the apparent advantages of the buffer state as a defensive device. In view of the increased speeds of land and air transport, it would seem that this type of defence is no longer a political or military advantage. The exceptionally rapid movement of Hitler's mechanized armies through Belgium would certainly suggest the inadequacy of the small buffer state. Normally such a unit has inadequate resources to maintain large standing armies or defences. At best it may retard an invasionary movement by land or air.

From the preceding discussion, it is apparent that the traditional concepts of political and military geo-strategy are based mainly upon the assumption that most human beings will travel either by land or by sea. In an air-age in which increasing numbers of people travel by plane in both peacetime and in war, the earlier concepts fail to apply or become relatively unimportant. Formerly impregnable installations such as Gibraltar have lost much of their strategic importance since they can now be immobilized by the application of sufficient air power, the use of long-range aircraft and destruction by thermonuclear weapons. Modern transportation has reduced the importance of the defence-in-depth tactics of former campaigns on land and has likewise destroyed the original effectiveness of devices such as buffer states.

Even the focal points of land and sea travel—the mountain passes, straits, or transportation corridors--in which movements have been channelled for centuries past become less significant in function as greater numbers of people travel by air.

It has been reported that the airlift between Japan and Korea from 1950 to 1953 transported more than a million passengers across the Korea Strait between the islands and the Asiatic mainland. In the campaign against the Japanese forces that were holding southern China in the 1940s, about 1,250,000 men were flown into China by "back door"—the Burma Road route over the "hump"—thereby going completely around any land fortifications or naval strong points that had been established by the Japanese army or navy. Their movement by air was opposed, of course, by units of the Japanese air forces, but the air travellers were not directly concerned at any time with traditional political or military geo-strategy of the lands or seas of south-eastern Asia.

Aerial warfare is free of most of the earth-bound restrictions imposed on military action that is land or sea-based. Although plenty of problems remain to be solved by further research and improved techniques, in general the airman has erased the major difficulties that plagued his progress in earlier years. Under normal circumstances of flight, for example, the aspects of reckoning distance and direction are done today by mechanical methods. Except for periods of take-off and landing when physical contact with the earth is necessary, the problem of poor flying weather has been eliminated because present planes follow courses well above weather disturbances of the lower atmosphere. Even the hazards of landing in poor weather have been largely eliminated by the present systems of directional signals and ground controls used for instrument flying. Excessively low air temperatures and pressures at great heights no longer represent serious problems because of technical improvements in equipment. Modern developments have so greatly increased the span of flight that frequent stops for refuelling are unnecessary, thus reducing (in effect) the number of air bases that must be maintained and defended. Further more, refuelling in the air is becoming a commonplace for military aircraft, promising further reduction in the number of contacts that airmen must make with land or sea. Even so, aircraft movements will never be wholly unrelated to the earth's surface and the competent and well-trained air officer must become thoroughly aware of the basic facts of geo-strategy.

These considerations with reference to the use of aircraft must involve a revision in the traditional approach to military geo-strategy, as suggested earlier. The impact of modern aircraft and their potentialities upon earlier concepts of geo-strategy is almost overwhelming in scope. The very concept of the conventional expression of speed in "miles per hour" begins to lose its meaning when flight is possible at speeds greater than the rate of earth rotation (about 1,000 miles per hour at the equator). The astonishingly rapid advances in the speeds and altitudes of air travel have brought belated recognition of factors far different from those traditionally associated with military strategy on sea or land. *It is now practical to reach any part of the world by long-range aircraft.* That single fact has brought radical change to all the principal military aspects of geo-strategy. To see what has come about, it is necessary to review the concepts set forth earlier in the light of present and forthcoming capabilities for long-distance flight.

THE THEORY OF DEFENCE IN-DEPTH

The long-standing idea (supported by the unsuccessful campaigns of Nepoleons and Hitlers) that a nation can secure itself against outside aggression or wait out an attack by retreating to a "hard core," "heartland," or other centrally-located arsenal of economic and military strength has been forcefully revised by present-day aviation accomplishments. The enormous mass movement of Russian heavy industry into the Siberian "heartland" when capture and destruction was threatened by German advances, was effective in 1941 and 1942. Today such a move would be a wasted effort, for any hostile power with modern aircraft and weapons could penetrate Siberia to any desired depth *if that power enjoyed air supremacy.* Even without complete air superiority, great damage could be done to military installations and factories in spite of all anti-aircraft defences that might be operating. *Distance from an active military engagement no longer provides defence for any people.*

There are, however, several aspects of mere size that provide some advantages when a nation is under attack by air. For one thing, some alight period of warning of the attack may be possible if aircraft detection devices such as radar installations can operate on a nation's frontiers some distance from its heart. Furthermore, a nation of great extent is in a favourable position to decentralize or disperse many of its industries, thus providing so many scattered targets that the most advanced methods of aerial attack—the use of thermonuclear weapons—cannot be used with greatest effectiveness.

Airpower can be extremely effective, however, if industrial centres are compactly arranged. When all the parts of an essential tool, for example, are produced within a small area or within short distances of each other, then a single high-potency bomb may destroy the entire production of the instrument. Destruction of one essential part would destroy the potentialities. Therefore the best defence against destruction of important industrial centres (in addition to a strong defensive air force) is to decentralize the entire manufacturing operation or parts of it.

The centre of any high industrial production area is peculiarly vulnerable to air attack and extremely difficult to defend against destruction. Some centres of activity cannot be decentralized for their protection, especially those places in which primary raw materials are produced and processed. Obviously there is no good solution to the problem of defending an important mining installation except to provide it with as much anti-aircraft strength as possible. The sources of raw materials cannot be decentralized but the manufacturing processes can be dispersed geographically. To accomplish this, a nation needs plenty of space within its borders. Therein lies almost the only remnant of the long-established theory of "defence-in-depth" as a military expedient.

> "Beyond merely limiting an enemy's use of land and sea spaces, air power's ability to use the air spaces gives it a supreme offensive capability the ability to penetrate. Unaffected by natural barriers, air forces operate in an environment of unlimited geographic range. Land massess, seas, rivers, mountains or man-made fortresses, barriers which have been the nemesis of surface forces since the beginning of warfare shrink to surface details of the terrain overflown far below. Modern long-range aircraft armed with the atomic (or hydrogen) bomb make vulnerable the entire spectrum of enemy targets, penetrating any land mass or ocean expanse with tremendous striking power (if air supremacy is on our side)... In the age of the atomic bomb and the airplane, we cannot expect the leisure to bring the enemy to terms by means of peripheral wars in which surface forces gradually claw their way into the enormous bulk of continental Eurasia (or any other land mass)."[1]

LOCATION AND STRATEGIC POSITION

Location on the earth's surface still affects military aviation activities and planning, although as the range of military aircraft increases, location becomes less significant to the flier. The large land masses of the northern hemisphere remain the principal theatre of air activity and strategy since they are the main concentrations of the world's population, resources and powerful political units. Location provides an element of convenience or of remoteness but inaccessibility and isolation as they were known before 1945 have disappeared from the face of the earth as far as military viewpoints are concerned. The great distance of New Zealand from the world's industrial and population centres is a matter of importance to the shipper, the immigrant, the trader and naval men ; *it is of little consequence to the military flier*, for it can be reached with ease in but a few hours of flying time.

Location behind the protection of barriers such as deserts, seas that are marginal to the continents, mountain masses, or beyond wide expanses of open sea formerly regarded as almost impregnable defences is no longer an advantage in a world where aircraft of great range can travel at rates of ten miles per minute or faster and refuel without the need of landing.

As early as 1944, it was beginning to become apparent that air power would shortly revise traditional concepts of the advantages of location. Spykman pointed out that seas adjacent to major land masses, under adequate air control, were of greater strategic importance than such massive war installations as those at Gibraltar or Singapore.[2] Since then, though the USA is still concerned in holding air supremacy over marginal seas (with air bases in northern Africa to control the terranean), it is recognized that the present long range of fighting aircraft has all but eliminated any advantages that formerly were believed inherent in the possession of strongly fortified bases placed strategically close to enemy borders. At the same time, air supremacy certainly can be maintained more easily if conveniently-located air bases are available.

To take a specific example of the changed attitudes towards a location that has been regarded as highly strategic ever since the rise of armed states in southern Europe, consider the position of Malta.

> "Throughout the whole of the Mediterranean campaign from 1940 till mid-1943 there was one dominating theme,

the ultimate aim the whole time was the same—to secure freedom to use the sea routes through and across the Mediterranean...Problem was difficult, because they only held points at each end of the 1,700 mile route and one point—Malta—at the centre. The key to their position in the whole Mediterranean lay in Malta. Thanks to the Cape and Takoradi routes, the forces in Egypt could at a price manage reasonably without the use of the Mediterranean route; but the retention of Malta was literally vital, not only to any possibility of denying the crossed route to the enemy but also to any prospects of reopening the through route.

"As an offensive base from which to operate naval and air forces against the enemy supply routes Malta was ideal. It was central. All the main ports of departure and arrival were within range of air reconnaissance ; from Malta, surface naval ships could operate under cover of darkness over a wide radius ; bomber and torpedo aircraft based on Malta could only be evaded by wide divergencies of the direct routes ; for submarines also it was an ideally situated base. But two dangers threatened it : firstly, direct destruction of the base itself by air attack and secondly, starving out the island by cessation of supply. Three times, when the use of Malta as an offensive base seriously threatened the maintenance of the Axis effort in Africa, did the Germany try to neutralise it by direct attack: early in 1941, again during the first quarter of 1942, and finally in the summer. Three times it failed to get that ultimate degree of air superiority which would have enabled it to deliver the 'coup-de-grace'."[3]

What the German attacks failed to accomplish at Malta on three occasions in 1941 and 1942 could be done today (assuming partial control of the air) with comparative ease. The 1,700-mile route with Malta as its central key point. would be a routine flight for long-range bombers; *one flight and one thermonuclear bomb would neutralize Malta's defences and strategic position and deny the use of the Mediterranean route to Western naval units.*

The effects of the changed attitudes towards strategic

position are already being felt. Since they can no longer be completely protected against air attack, it seems futile to continue to maintain massive land or naval forces and installations in any great degree of strength at strategic locations such as Singapore, Pearl Harbour, Panama, Gibraltar, Suez, Dakar, Formosa, Aden, Ceylon, Malta, Manila, Cyprus or Diego Garcia. Fortification, repair facilities, air bases, drydocks and similar installations will continue to be needed at advantageous locations but their main defences need to be directed against air attack. Any hostile move against them from either land or sea would be subject to control from the air ; a hostile attack against them from the air could be defeated by superior air power.

Most of the significant locations on land or sea—foci of rail transport, impregnable land fortifications, roads through mountain passes and other strategic focal points—described in earlier chapters are of decreasing importance in military aviation. They represent bombing targets that are to be destroyed in order to attain military objectives such as interruption of rail shipments, interference with troop movement or destruction of repair facilities or enemy air bases. But in themselves they can offer no real resistance to air attack ; they only provide targets of superior quality upon which the full force of air power can be expended in a minimum time and with maximum results—always upon the assumption that the attacking force has air supremacy.

BOUNDARIES, BOUNDARY ZONES AND BUFFER STATES

Important as the placing of political boundaries may be in defining the physical limits of a nation, those boundaries are of minor importance to the military aviator as long as his course lies over neutral or friendly territory. In Western Europe, for example, where a sovereign nation such as Belgium (11,779 square miles) is only a little larger than Maryland (USA ; 10,577 square miles), the present air speeds permit the whole country to be crossed in fifteen minutes or less and the pilot at high attitudes is hardly aware that he has utilized the airspace of Belgium before he had entered that of its neighbour. This is true, of course, only as long as he remains west of the Communist nations. He must necessarily be cognizant of and recognize the position of the borders of hostile nations ; to violate them either purposefully or unwittingly might lead to many repercussions, both personal and international.

In general, the higher the latitude and the faster the flight, the less importance attaches to the political boundaries of friendly nations. In future, proper recognition of this fact may lead to de-emphasis of certain present features of political boundaries such as heavy land fortifications. As suggested earlier, the main objective in establishing buffer states has already been eliminated. They represent a political relic of wars fought on land, and except that they force an attacking air power to send its planes at slightly greater distance in order to effect deep penetration, they serve no military function today. It should be recalled, however, that buffer states do contribute labour and raw materials to that nation whose satellites they become.

AIR POWER IN RELATION TO GEOGRAPHY

The advent of massive air power since the close of World War II demands a reassessment of military air transport in relation to geography. Air power has changed the values of size, location, focal points, international boundaries and other traditional aspects of political geography. To discuss the matter further, however, requires a statement of the meaning of the term and this has been done by the United States Air Force authorities as follows (in part) :

> *Air Power*, that power that "arises from man's ability to fly aircraft..." existing in a particular nation, "adapted to military ends, as in an air force or the power to deliver an air attack,"... ; *a nation having predominant strength in civilian and military aviation.*

Obviously the geographical foundations of air power are mainly contained in the italicized part of the definition ; the *results* of air strength are expressed in the ability to wage successful air war. It is apparent that the development of air power cannot materially effect basic geographical conditions such as relief of the land, climate, location or most natural resources but it can deny access to raw materials and resources. At the conclusion of a successful application of air power, this force can affect the extent of land under control of a nation (that is, the area or sphere of political influence) as the combined air and naval forces were able to "shrink" Japan's control over a maximum land area of 1½ million square miles as of July, 1942, to minimum of 145,000 square miles in August, 1945.

Successful use of air power is able to make profound alterations in details of the geographical landscape. While air attack did not eradicate the city of Hamburg in July and August of 1943, it did destroy one-third of all the dwellings in the city, radically changing the aspects of the urban landscape and destroying the normal operation and functions of the city and its port area. Throughout all of Germany, 20 per cent of dwelling units were destroyed or damaged and 7,500,000 people were made homeless. In Japan, two-thirds of the structures in the city of Hiroshima were rendered unusable by one bomb. Bridges, tunnels, transport facilities, power installations, reservoirs and dams can be completely put out of operation or eliminated by air attack ; air power is a potent agent of geographical change.

Not only can it change the landscape, detail but air power can change the capacity of a nation for waging war successfully. One-fourth of Hiroshima's industrial capacity was destroyed by the first atomic bomb ; only the fact that many of the city's war plants were on the outskirts of the community prevented a much greater proportion of damage. In Germany, output of aviation gasoline fell, as the result of Allied bombardment of synthetic oil plants, from a maximum production of 316,000 tons monthly to a trickle of only 5,000 tons. This acute shortage of gasoline was, in turn, responsible for Germany's inability to provide adequate training for her pilots, whereupon "the deterioration of quality of German pilots appears to be the most important single cause of the defeat of the German Air Force."[4]

The interference of effective air power with the wartime economy appears in an analysis of the results of bombing. Before 1939, Germany depended on imports of 70 per cent of her iron ore, 83 per cent of copper, 75 per cent of natural rubber, 66 per cent of petroleum, and all of her manganese, chromite, nickel, wolfram (a source of tungsten). The nation experienced no serious shortage of any of the above (except for oil in 1942) until 1944, when long range bombers were able to penetrate deeply into the hearts of the German industrial centres and destroy the oil plants and other factories. Steel and coal shortages never did exist, although electric power shortage and the aerial bombing of transportation facilities did disrupt the distribution systems. Not the shortage of raw materials but the destruction of her industry was the decisive factor in Germany's defeat.

By the middle of 1944, as the direct result of the bombing of German war plants, the aviation gasoline potential was 90 per cent destroyed ; only half of other petroleum products were available ; steel production was cut in half. The destruction of German railways and canals, as already noted, led to stagnation of coal and other shipments. By March, 1945, coal deliveries were down to 4 per cent below normal and synthetic rubber production had declined to 62 per cent, and nitrate production was only half of normal.[5]

"The German experience suggests that even a first class military power-rugged and resilient as Germany was, cannot live long under full scale and free exploitation of air weapons over the heart of its territory......"[6]

The effect of air power on Japan's industrial potential was no less striking. Although (due to military policy) there was little destruction of Japanese jail facilities, electric power plants or finished war material (which was largely stored underground), the USA did destroy 470,000 barrels of petroleum products, 221,000 tons of foodstuffs and 2 billion yards of textiles. The USA's aerial bombing reduced Japan's industrial production capacity by[7] :

83 per cent of oil refinery output
75 per cent of aircraft engine parts manufacture
60 per cent of air-frame plant production
70 per cent of electronics and communication equipment
30 per cent of army ordnance plant output
28 per cent of naval ordnance plant output
15 per cent merchant and naval shipyards
35 per cent light metals capacity
15 per cent ingot steel production, and
10 per cent chemicals production.

And all this was accomplished mainly by the use of conventional bombs and bombing methods, before the overpowering destructiveness of the atomic bomb. Japan's industrial and urban geography underwent radical changes in a very brief time as the result of effective air power exercised by the United States.

> "Control of the air was essential to the success of every major military operation...The first objective of all commanders in the Pacific war, whether ground, sea or air, whether American, Allied or Japanese, was to assure control of the air."

This was achieved by air power that consisted of the planes and pilots, plus *all* the sources of strength that supported the control of the air including close coordination of air, sea and land operations. The control by Allied air power was so complete that Japan was forced to use suicide (kamikaze) attacks in a last desperate effort to regain air supremacy.

> "Heavy, sustained and accurate attack against carefully selected targets is required to produce decisive results when attacking an enemy's sustaining resources...For the future it is important fully to grasp the fact that enemy planes enjoying control of the sky over one's head can be as disastrous to one's country as its occupation by physical invasion."[8]

Potential air power cannot be destroyed since its basis lies in the geo-strategy that is the foundation of national power, population factors, standards of research and development, financial condition, poverty or wealth of natural resources, political conditions ; all these and other elements as well lie behind potential air power.

> "The following are suggested as the principal conditions and elements which, over a long period of time, will contribute to or limit the air power available for national objectives, either the normal civil objectives of peace or the military objectives of emergency of war :
>
> (1) Geographic and geo-strategic conditions including location, extent, physical conformation, climate and weather, of the national territory and its dependencies.
> (2) Resources including economic and material resources in national territory and available elsewhere.
> (3) Population including size, temperament, general educational level and adaptability for aeronautics (flying, aircraft manufacturing, and allied industries).
> (4) Industrial development including the general national technological level, as well as manufacturing, engineering and research available or adaptable for aeronautics.
> (5) Political conditions including national incentives, government policies and national aeronautical right.[9]

In order to capitalize on the strengths inherent in air power as a weapon in its own right, it is imperative that control of the air be maintained in such degree that an attacking force is unable to destroy material resources or large numbers of the population. This requires constant vigilance and increasing development of all those factors that support air power. In this light, the following statement by General Karl Koller, Chief of the German Air Staff, 1944-45, reveals the views of a commander who saw the results of Germany's loss of air supremacy at first hand.

"We have lost the war....There are many reasons why Germamy lost the war : political, economic and military reasons which were our own fault. None of these reasons were decisive in themselves nor were they together decisive ...The campaigns in Poland, Holland, Belgium, France and Norway had proved unequivocally how important air supremacy is in a modern war...Not Germany who showed what superior air forces and skill in leading them mean, learned the lesson, but on the contrary the enemy countries who drew the proper and logical conclusions and with an iron tenacity built up a superior air force which alone could lead to victory.

"As long as we had air supremacy, nobody interfered with our shipping in the North Sea, along the German coast and from Holland to Brest, Bordeaux and Spain. The British Fleet did not show itself ; no noticeable traffic dared to enter the Channel and they often hardly dared to go into the southern part of the Irish Sea and everything was forced to the far north. As long as we had air supremacy, nobody threatened our industries or the peaceful life of our homeland ; our lines of communication in the Mediterranean were not interfered with. If our air supremacy had been kept up right from the beginning..., we would not have been defeated in Africa or in the Mediterranean area.... But the political leadership in Germany, in its short-sightedness and in complete misjudgement of the tenacity and mentality of the Anglo-Saxons and the potential war power of the United States in the background, had believed that the war in the west had already been won in 1940 and started out on the folly of the Russian war....

"we were smothered by the enormous superiority of American and Russian material because the German High Command undertook too much on the ground in the East and because it did not direct the main weight of armament right from the beginning towards air supremacy and thereby safeguard Germany's vital zones and armament industry and ward off any attack from the West. Everything depends on air supremacy."[10]

One major additional element enters this picture. Air power is an instrument of large proportions, flexible and adaptable to defensive or offensive warfare. It also serves a very special purpose in that it is the most effective device by which the most advanced instruments of wartime destruction, the atomic, hydrogen or cobalt bombs can be delivered within enemy territory where they can be counted upon to demoralize the wartime activities of any nation. This single fact justifies the development of long-range bombers as a leading component of air power, in order that the means of delivering such weapons shall be instantaneously available when an air offensive is necessary. The mere existence of long-range bombers plus thermonuclear weapons is a most powerful deterrent to aggressive military action and international outlawry. Given the combination of five long-range bombers and five hydrogen bombs and a base from which to operate and return in the hands of a hostile power, New York, Thule, Pearl Harbour, Detroit or Washington might cease to exist unless the USA has air power and air supremacy with which to defend her cities and industries.

> "American air power could deny Red Armies' freedom of movement, pound them continuously and destroy their supplies. In no other way, USA has the manpower, means and economic capabilities to cope with the USSR's natural allies Resources, Distance, Winter and Manpower.... What is clear is that if war comes, USA's only hope of victory lies in the prompt achievement of over-whelming air supremacy. Moreover, air supremacy is the best war deterrent because it can destroy the enemy war potential.... It is therefore suicidal for the United States not to direct its vast industrial potential into full-scale production to provide the best air force in the world. If it fails to do this and permits air supremacy to rest in Soviet hands, the USSR could destroy the military potential of the United States, such a disaster would be the death of freedom everywhere."[11]

Official recognition of the USA's need of strong air control appears in the report of the President's Air Policy Commission. The United States.

> "...can be supreme in the air by the weight or our air power...and can build a Military Establishment which will keep up with any nation and be a powerful force for peace. In our opinion, this Military Establishment must be built around the air arm.... Our military security must be based on air power...."

Heretofore the United States has been able to make most of its preparations for war after war began, but

> "there is a new element through which this country may be attacked the air.... This means that the traditional peace-time strategy of the United States must be changed radically," that is, "to have in peacetime a force in being which will protect to the greatest extent possible our air space as well as our water approaches."[12]

In conclusion, it should be stressed that geo-strategic thinking should be revised in the light of present technical accomplishments (the great range for military aircraft, plus the force of thermonuclear weapons and pilotless aircraft) to take full account of the potentialities and the prospects are far from favourable for us unless we are aware of our needs and alert to the fact that "air power will, in wars to come, remain the sharp edge of a nation's total fighting power."

REFERENCES

1. Anonymous, "The Power to penetrat," Air University Quarterly Review 6 : 2 31. Winter, 1953-54.
2. Nicholas Spykman, *Geography of the Peace*, Harcourt Grace and Company, New York, 1944, pp. 54-55.
3. Marshal of the Royal Air Force, The Loid Tedder, G.C.B., *Air Power in War*, Hodder and Stoughten, London 1947, pp. 72-74.
4. United States Strategic Bombing Survey, *Overall Report, European War*, Washington, D.C., September 30, 1945 p. 22-
5. *Ibid.*, pp 35-52.

6. United States Strategic Bombay Survey, *Summary Report*, *European War*, Washington, D.C., September 30, 1945, p. 16.
7. United States Strategic Bombing Survey. Summary Report, Pacific War, Washington D.C., July 1, 1946, p. 18.
8. *Ibid.*, pp. 27-28.
9. J.C. Cooper, Air Power, *Air Affairs* 1 : 89. September, 1946.
10. Extract from the Members of General Karl Koller, Chief of the German Air Staff, 1944-45, in *Air Power* 1 : 365-369, Spring, 1954.
11. General Bonner Fellers, U.S. Army (Ret), "*A Look at War*,' Air university Quarterly Review. 6 : 14-24, winter, 1953-54.
12. July 18, 1947, quoted in Straus- Hape and Possony, pp. 628-34.

CHAPTER FIVE

GEOLOGY AND NATIONAL POWER

Geology has played its part in all wars from those in which the crude stone hammer was the principal weapon down to the present war wherein all sciences contributing to mastery of air, land or sea, are being utilized to their fullest degree.

It is unfortunate that persons who have had no training in or contact with the field of geology, do not properly appreciate its greatest usefulness. Geologists themselves have been slow to organize an educational geologic programme to augment the military and naval services of the country and the latter have been slow in making immediate adequate use of the important knowledge which the science of geology and the country's trained geologists can supply.

This neglect on the part of geologists has been matched by a general ignorance of or indifference to geology by military and naval officials ; and by the tendency of other types of technicians—geophysicists, engineers, geographers, meteorologists, etc—to assume that geology is a minor adjunct of their own field.

The strategic worth of economic and topographic geology may be evaluated by its general application to the following activities which are of vital importance in wartime.

(A) Interpretation of terrain for military purposes.
(B) Conversion of ground for military manoeuvres.

(C) Maintenance of supplies and communications.

(D) Miscellaneous geologic applications.

(E) Expansion of normal domestic geologic activities.

A. INTERPRETATION OF TERRAIN FOR MILITARY MANOEUVRES

Although modern warfare is exceedingly complex, it is basically a series of manoeuvres for and upon portions of the earth's crust land, sea and air. In so far as it involves activity upon the land, it is occupying an arena that has been and is now the subject of intensified study by the geologist and common sense recommends that an expert on that arena be consulted.

Several examples will be listed wherein even without special military training, the competent geologist can contribute opinions of weight and matters of fact.

(*1*) *Analyses of terrain for troop movement, attack and defence*. The field geologist has intimate knowledge of the processes that produce earth features. Better than any other technician, he can analyse a terrain, appreciate its topography and understand its contours. This ability is a function of his particular training and with it a geologist is equipped to make complete and rapid analyses of the ground. He can do this from observation, from maps, from photographs or from another's description.

(*2*) *Interpretation of unknown topography from geologic literature, photographs and published geologic maps* : Constantly the geologist is required to make detailed interpretations of conditions of topography and geology in regions that he has never seen. Such requirement is part of his academic training and later becomes an integral item of his personal experience. There is probably no other technician who has an equal ability to visualize these conditions from maps and documents. Given access to published literature, a corps of trained field geologists could operate from a Delhi office to give better geologic and geographic advice about the character of unknown terrain than an observant native of the region under study.

Furthermore, there is probably no major portion of the

earth's surface that has not been examined on the ground by some living geologist now resident in the USA ; and for most areas of the globe, an American geologist can be found who knows the country intimately, its contours, climate, resouices and even its language.

(3) *Appraisal of mineral producing regions or objectives, their types, values, accessibility and military importance* : This is the specific field of the trained geologist who is fully accustomed to the survey, appraisal and interpretation of natural mineral resources. It is likely that there are no important mineral deposits in the world which some resident American geologist has not visited or about which first-hand information as to type, value and reserves, is not readily available.

To mention a few specific examples : There are probably a score of petroleum geologists who are wholly conversant from recent experience with the oil fields of Borneo, Sumatra or Java. American geologists and engineers are personally familiar with all important mineral operations of Central and South America.

(4) *Fluid appraisal of foreign or enemy mineral resources* : It is important to have a fluid appraisal of the changing character of foreign or enemy mineral resources and as already indicated, the geologists is in a position to keep abreast of these changes.

(5) *Fluid interpretations of relative vulnerability in terms of topography, mineral and water supply and general accessibility* : In matters of both tactics and strategy, the fluid appraisal of these matters must currently be given careful study. Probably no previous war has so fully vindicated the need of constant interpretation of changing conditions in the light of new developments. The fortifications of Singapore, Hong Kong, the Maginot and Mannerheim lines are the product of 1918 strategy. Their strategic importance could well have been different if the last two decades of military science had placed more emphasis on the geologic aspects of the land.

(6) *Interpretation analysis of current geologic problems encountered during military campaigns* : Here again the geolo-

gist should be consulted to furnish current, fluid interpretations of situations that may be progressively changing.

(*7*) *Selection of testing areas to simulate terrains of possible campaigns* : Since the war is worldwide, no portion of the earth's surface may escape free from it and every actual type of terrain is involved—the glaciated areas of high mountains and high latitudes, the jungle as well as the desert areas, the hinterland and the coastline. Indeed, the latter is a subject of specialization in itself. Coastlines are quite variable and are different where the sea is transgressing from where it is regressing. The geologist is able to advise as to testing grounds that will duplicate conditions of anticipated campaigns and can there give counsel in the testing and use of men and equipment destined to enter combat in specific environmental conditions.

(*8*) *Actual reconnaissance* : The geologist should be employed in reconnaissance in advance of occupation of territory ; he should be prepared to make current geologic surveys of it during occupation ; and should carefully study any territory to be relinquished, in all three instances being able to provide information of military value.

(*9*) Analysis of shore features to determine coastal conditions of beach, off-hore depth and landing or siege conditions.

(*10*) Interpretation of climate, soil, vegetation and terrain in terms of living conditions, sustenance and occupation.

(*11*) Appraisal of sites for roads, encampments, mines, batteries, airdromes and other semi-permanent installations.

(*12*) Solution of many problems dealing with the conversion of ground for military use as discussed below.

Most of these functions need little or no specific explanation at this point ; they are simple obvious points where the applications of geologic principles and practice are patently of considerable importance.

B. CONVERSION OF GROUND FOR MILITARY USE

In the conversion or adaptation of ground for military use,

geology becomes a pre-requisite to engineering, and skilled geologic advice is a vital necessity in virtually every phase of this work. Many of the items listed below will be claimed by the engineer as his field ; yet he will have to call upon his own geologic training, often inadequate and at best woefully meagre, to solve the problems raised. Civilian activities of most geologists with the pursuit of their profession provides the background to step into service in many of the following categories and there should be no difficulty in finding geologists now who can serve the armed forces along these lines with little or no military training necessary.

It would be possible to considerably enlarge each of the particular geologic problems connected with the following topics and any trained geologist is competent to do so. It should also be noted that nearly all of the following listed items have both a positive and a negative aspect, namely, a side dealing with construction, use and offensive purpose and a side dealing with demolition, prevention and defensive purpose. Geology is of assistance on both sides.

(1) Construction of trenches, fortifications, artificial impediments, munition dumps, earthworks and similar installations.
(2) Construction of airdromes, runways, shelters, foundations, etc.
(3) Blasting, tunnelling, mining and quarrying.
(4) Construction or prevention of rock or earth slides, slopes, rock cuts and similar excavaions.
(5) Reclamation ot swamps, marshes, quicksands, etc.
(6) Flooding, drainage, construction of dams, levees, canals, reservoirs, wells, etc.

In all of these activities, the civilian geologist is commonly consulted and his advice is basically responsible for the engineering success of many of these projects. Seemingly his advice should be as eagerly made use of in analogous military operations on the success of which a far greater outcome may rest than any civilian operation.

The geologist should be employed to assist in making the

original location ; to give advice concerning the topographic advantages of the site chosen ; to advise regarding the character of earth handled, the depth of overburden, methods of excavation required, available construction materials, drainage properties of rock and soil, strength of foundations, type of surfacing needed, reaction of explosives ; and he should be consulted in the protective or defensive demolition of previously constructed installations.

(7) Stability, strength, character and workability of any given ground of material.

In determining these important factors, the geologist can give quicker and more reliable aid than any other technician.

(8) Reclamation of shelled territory, rock fragmentation through bombardment, etc.
(9) Utilisation of caves and caverns ; operation and exploration of mines and other underground workings.
(10) Conversion of local mineral industries for military use.

It should not be necessary to amplify the above topics in order to reveal the importance that geology has at each point.

C. MAINTENANCE OF SUPPLIES AND COMMUNICATIONS

In civilian life, the entire field of mineral detection, prospecting, discovery and appraisal, falls in the area of geologic science as well as many allied problems of mineral recovery and development. Specially trained geologists are now available to do similar necessary service in military life. For example.

(1) Prospecting and reconnaissance for supplies of road metal, brick clay, raw stone, marl ballast, sand, material for concrete and other native materials of potential military use.

One whole side of military activity must deal with the maintenance of supplies indicated above, for which the geologist is better prepared to search and exploit than other technicians.

(2) Drilling, excavations and quarrying for the immediate use of the above materials.

(3) Hydrologic problems, ground water, springs, etc.

Another broad field for the geologist is that of ground and surface water, the location of wells, determinations of source of springs, water supply, filtration of water and permeability of rock and soil, depth of water tables, source of ground water, underground water storage, etc.

(4) Location and construction of roads.

In the location of construction of military roads or other lines of transportation, the supervision of location, selection of ballast, types of road construction, etc., the geologist can render as adequate military service as he has long been doing in similar civilian activities.

D. MISCELLANEOUS GEOLOGIC APPLICATIONS

There are numerous other categories in which the geologist, because of his general training or because of certain specific specialization or experience, can perform valuable functions not usually considered. These points may be briefly listed without special elaboration.

(1) The magnetic detection of mines, pipes, metallic underground installations and other geophysical service.

(2) The construction and detection of camouflage should be definitely in the geological field, for the geologist is better acquainted with the appearance of the ground than anyone else.

(3) Matters of sanitation and burial are closely allied to the geologic problems of underground drainage.

(4) Gas retention in rock and soil.

(5) Restoration of captured or damaged installations such as oil wells, mines, etc.

(6) General map making and surveying.

(7) Scouting and general reconnaissance. It should be noted here that the field geologist is an experienced hand in getting about under adverse conditions with a minimum of equipment, and under conditions where resourcefulness is a necessary asset.

E. EXPANSION OF NORMAL DOMESTIC GEOLOGIC ACTIVITIES

Finally, the manifold activities of geologists in general civilian affairs need to be specially geared to the war effort. Some of these duties take on new applications no less important than the active military applications listed above. These things, as well, should be given careful thought.

(1) Continued and more intensive search for strategic or essential mineral deposits.

(2) Evaluation of known low-grade or normally non-commercial supplies of critical raw materials. (Example ; manganese, zinc, iron ore, etc.).

(3) Experimentation with substitution of unused resources of value as replacements for materials now exhausted. (Example; high alumina clays).

(4) Geologic advice on engineering problems of domestic defence, new military and industrial installations, roads, dams, wells, foundations, airdromes, camps, etc.

(5) Assembling of maps, geologic literature and appraisal of geologic opinion concerning other possible applications of geology to the needs of the armed forces.

(6) Instruction at service schools and preparation of textbooks on military geology.

(7) Preparation of military guide books and maps.

(8) Reorganization of geologic courses taught in colleges and universities so as to further the dissemination of knowledge of matters of geologic importance.

(9) Reorganization of existing geologic societies and agencies into the most effective cooperation with military and naval authorities.

(10) Continued reiteration of the practical value of geology in both war and peace.

Hence an organization should be contemplated, if not now set up, so as to make the most practical use of this science both in the post-war settlement and in possible future military or naval undertakings.

CHAPTER SIX

BASES OF NATIONAL POWER

RESOURCES

Although an adequate supply of minerals and metals is absolutely essential in conducting modern warfare, there must, in addition, be adequate supplies of food and plenty of labour to do the work of preparing for and maintaining active war effort.

A specific definition of the non-Communist world nations and the Communist nations is desirable at this point and this definition has been held to throughout this book. For the non-Communist world, production figures have been included for the United States, Canada, France, India, Italy, Australia, Turkey, Pakistan, the United Kingdom, Brazil, Mexico, the Union of South Africa, Japan and some of the smaller nations. The Communist nations include the Soviet Union, China, Rumania, Hungary, Czechoslovakia and Poland only.

In spite of the obvious temporary character of the political alignment above, it is only by surveys of this type that we are able to determine in what manner our economic potential should be reinforced and in what respective directions economy is relatively strong.

FOODSTUFFS

Foods represent an essential item in military planning since a constant and adequate supply is necessary if the energies of any nation are to be devoted to successful war operations, either offensive or defensive. The principal food-grain staples of the world are wheat, corn and rice in the mid-latitudes and subtropical realm. Minor food crops include rye, barley, millet, oats and some others of secondary importance. Luxury commodities that are not essential to human existence and nutrition, such as tea, coffee, bananas and citrus fruits have been excluded from this survey.

The United States leads in production of wheat among all the nations, with the Soviet Union as a second country. The United States is far ahead of any competitors in corn production, outstripping China her nearest competitor, ten-fold. China produces the greatest amount of rice than India, her nearest competitor. Japan and Pakistan are about equal in production, occupying third place jointly. The Soviet Union is the greatest producer of rye, growing four times the amount of the next largest producer, Poland. The United States leads in production of oats with twice as much as the Soviet Union in spite of the decline in the use of the horse in farm operations in this country. China produces the largest amount of barley, but as in the case of wheat, rice and millet, the population is so great that almost all grain produced must be consumed at home, leaving no surplus available for trade. The other important food supply derived from plants is the sugar crop. The non-Communist world produces more than 15 million metric tons of cane and beet sugar compared to 4½ million metric tons produced within the Communist nations.

Well-rounded diets normally should include some protein and fat materials derived from animal sources. The world's animal foods come principally from four sources : cattle, swine, sheep and fish. It should be noted, however, that these creatures provide far more than food since they serve dual purposes. Cattle provide not only meat and daily goods but also hides and a wide variety of other materials for manufacture. Swine are used mainly for food but sheep provide wool in addition to meat.

Although India is the largest producer of cattle, most of her production is non-commercial and from the standpoint of her contribution to the world's food supply or to her own needs, India's cattle production is almost entirely consumed within. But at present, India is exporting large quantities of meat and animal products to Arab countries. The United States raised about one-half as many cattle as India, followed closely by production of the Soviet Union. China is the largest grower of swine, but like her rice production, this food must be used for her own people and there is no surplus to spare or to share. Commercially the United States leads in growing hogs, with the Soviet Union growing about half as many as the USA does. Australia is far ahead in numbers of sheep, with the Soviet Union growing about one-half the Australian production, followed in order by Argentina, India and the United States. Japan has the largest catch of fish and also consumes much of her production. The United States is second and Norway third. In this protein food, the non-Communist world is far ahead of the Communist nations.

CRITICAL MATERIALS OTHER THAN FOOD AND MINERALS

Supplied with adequate food, it is essential that any nation involved in a military dispute should also be supplied with goods which can be converted into machinery and the material of war. Almost twice as much cotton is grown in the United States as is grown by her nearest competitor, the Soviet Union. India is third in production, followed by Egypt and China. Wool is produced in greatest quantity by Australia, with the Soviet Union, Argentina and India following closely. Soyabeans are grown in about equal quantities in the United States and China, with the former leading slightly. No other nations compete in soyabean production. The Communist nations lead in hemp and flax (fibre) with the Soviet Union far ahead in both. Jute is almost a monopoly of India with Bangladesh second.

For 50 years, rubber has been a vital necessity in wartime because of the increasing mechanization. During World War I (1914-1918), the use of rubber-tired vehicles was beginning to be important but for practical purposes, the USA was able to obtain rubber in needed quantities without undue difficulty or shortages. At that time, it was a commodity that was obtained mainly in the wild state from the interior parts of the Amazon basin in Brazil. In World War II, the pattern was wholly different, with the largest rubber supplies coming from plantation sources in Malaya and the East Indies.

> "Up to World War II, the United States was dependent on outside sources, principally south-east Asia, for its entire new rubber supply. This was all natural rubber. Synthetic rubber production capacity developed during the war but much of it was closed down afterwards, to be reopened after the invasion of South Korea."
>
> "In view of the United States ability to expand synthetic rubber capacity, no serious security supply problem need be encountered during the next 25 years. The national rubber stockpile, at goal level, would presumably provide supplementary supplies during the build-up period. The stockpile goal can, of course, be adjusted to changes in the relative dependence on imports, and to changes in the degree of substitutability as between natural and synthetic rubbers. Further the stockpile goal would be affected by the extent to which natural rubber production is successfully fostered in Central and South America and in Africa."
>
> "Should natural rubber production fail to expand significantly, the United States and other non-Communist countries should increase synthetic rubber production at a correspondingly greater rate and thus be closer to the plant capacity levels that might be required in a war emergency."[1]

Lumber worth 620 million cubic metres[2] is produced by the non-Communist world, with only 340 million cubic metres normally produced by the Communist countries in spite of the fact that Siberian forests contain enormous untapped quantities of this important resource (though admittedly the quality of much of the lumber obtainable from the taiga lands is of substandard quality). Though the advantage in production of this commodity lies with the non-Communist world, the United States and the Soviet Union are about evenly matched, with Brazil and Canada taking third and fourth places. The non-Communist world is well ahead of the Communist world in supplies of cotton, synthetic rubber, wool, jute and lumber and is evenly matched with the Communist nations in soyabean production. It is extremely short on the supply of hemp and flax to be used for fibre, though with sufficient inducement there is no reason why these crops could not be produced successfully outside the Soviet Union, and in large quantity. Other commodities in which the non-Communist world is well supplied, include cottonseed, olive oil, rayon, abaca, raw silk and newsprint.

At this point, one main fact should be stressed : raw materials that may be critical (from the military standpoint) at one period in history may not be of great importance at other period. To illustrate the point, reference to an article by Robert B. Hall, written at the outbreak of World War II early in 1940,[3] classifies 17 "strategic" materials as follows.

TABLE 6.1

The Seventeen Strategic Materials

Priority I	Priority II	Priority III
Antimony	Mica	Aluminium
Chromium	Quicksilver	Coconut shell char
Manganese	Tungsten	Optical glass
Manila hemp		Wool
Nickel		
Quartz crystal		
Quinine		
Rubber		
Silk		
Tin		

In the light of experiences in World War II, the list needs considerable revision to bring it down to date. Six of the 17 items can be dropped : manila hemp, quinine, rubber, silk, coconut shell char and optical glass. Under wartime pressures, the USA developed strong synthetic fibres that can replace (for most uses) manila hemp and silk. Atabrine and other substitutes have relieved the USA of complete dependence upon quinine in the treatment of tropical diseases. Synthetic rubber, as noted above, may replace natural rubber in an emergency. Coconut shell char (used in gas masks in World War I) has several substitutes and the USA's production of optical glass has greatly advanced in the last 30 years.

"Strategic" materials that would be needed in quantity to support a modern war effort would surely include petroleum, uranium and thorium, titanium, and for the United States, iron ore, manganese, chromite and tin.

THE LABOUR FORCE

Inert material wealth must be transformed into articles of greatest usefulness at home or abroad into machinery, implements, fabrics, foods in time of peace and into weapons in time of war. To accomplish this transformation, large numbers of people must be available to do the work above and beyond the personnel necessary to undertake active war operations or provide replacements.

Most labourers in the Communist realm are employed in agricultural pursuits directed towards sufficient food for themselves ; relatively few are engaged in factory work, though the Soviet Union has been greatly expanding its manufacturing capacity for the past 30 years. The significant item to note is that Soviet industry has been growing rapidly and will probably continue to do so. At present, India is significantly growing very rapidly and it is estimated that within 10 years, it will become one of the most powerful nations of the world.

On the other hand, the four Western nations have large numbers of employees engaged in manufacturing, though agriculture is by no means neglected ; this provides a more favourable economic balance in the West than in the East.

The total number of people are an important factor in waging war. At this point the situation looks favourable to the non-Communist world in terms of population and of area. Many of the people on both sides are backward, living primitive lives with very low living standards ; they cannot be counted on to produce as much or more than they need for themselves. Further, much of the land surface of the earth is ill-suited to produce any quantity of food or other materials with which to carry on successful modern warfare.

The strength of a nation today is based not only upon its wealth of raw materials but in large part upon the abilities and numbers of its people. A most important consideration in time of military activity is the effectiveness and amount of factory labour . Without a productive organization to supply the needed quantity and quality of goods to the military, there can be no efficient fighting force. Modern warfare demands factory methods of the most advanced type. There was a time in our history when the illiterate Indian ironworker could produce a rifle or high quality weapon for the soldier of the first war of independence in 1857, but modern war operates on a very different basis and the production of such goods must take every possible advantage of modern technological and mechanical skills in order to have sufficient material to supply a fighting organization.

The most efficient type of factory labour is normally obtained when the work is done on a basis of pride of craftsmanship. The reduction of as many operations as possible to a mechanical state and attempts to use labourers who have little sympathy with the political or military regime, will provide an unsatisfactory labour supply. In other words, the ability to adapt to the extensive use of machinery, the assembly line and mechanized transport under good working conditions, is the best way to obtain large and steady output of goods at low cost per unit of production. This applies to factory labour, to farm labour and other activities where the final product is not highly processed. It applies also to the fabrication of intricate tools and the like but, in addition, these also require a high degree of intelligence to be effective, whether used in their manufacture or in their performance.

Staging successful modern warfare also involves the operation of a fighting machine of large proportions and the development of such an organization is seldom possible unless there is a strong will on the part of the citizens to establish and maintain such an operation. The so-called unskilled labourer in the factory is as poor a worker for the state as is the conscript in the military organization who is forced into military activity against his will. Neither is in a position to perform to the utmost of his ability, and such workers are serious liabilities in any organization. A successful military organization necessarily involves the ultimate in team work and to a certain extent the subordination of the individual. Any nation whose people are unable to fit themselves into such a pattern of activity, is not in a position to undertake military operations on a large scale. The adaptability of both civilian and man in uniform to the requirements of staging and successfully completing a military engagement may determine the outcome of the war effort. The idea is frequently expressed by the use of the term "morale" but that word does not entirely express the situation.

The toughness of a people also is a matter of some consequence whether it be ability to endure long working hours on an assembly line to maintain farming operations with inadequate labour and machinery or the physical stamina needed to undertake long-distance flight. Unless both citizen and military man are able to make certain necessary sacrifices of time and strength in order to achieve success, the chances of winning a modern war are slight indeed.

In addition to the foregoing, it is essential that any people undertaking to wage modern war should be reasonably united in thought as well as in action. Internal dissension is a weakening process whether it be in a factory or among the members of a bomber crew. This does not necessarily mean that all individuals should be in complete agreement but it does mean that no individual shall be so out of sympathy with the group activities that he attempts to defeat its purpose either by direct or indirect methods. Here again the word "morale" is suggested, but since it is a word difficult to define, the expression "unity of thought and action" is generally more satisfactory. No nation can afford to have its house divided in time of war ; neither should there be serious division in time of peace.

Modern warfare also calls for a considerable degree of ingenuity. People who are in no position to make constant improvements in machines, methods, weapons or in matters of mere daily routine, are certainly in no position to defend themselves, let alone undertake any offensive action of a military nature. Present-day war demands a high degree of ingenuity on the part of the people who are producing goods and on the part of those who are expending them. People have not devised a substitute for cleverness and good judgement.

As indicated earlier, the size of the total population becomes a deciding factor in determining strengths or weaknesses of a particular nation. In spite of all the mechanization of wartime and peacetime machinery, it is still necessary to use large numbers of people if not actually under arm, then as producers, capable of maintaining the necessary flow of supplies. Recent wars have involved the use of almost all available manpower in one way or another and nations have even begun to utilize women in essential industries during war. A few nations, including India, Israel and the United States, have also put small numbers of women in uniform, using them to release men for more active duty.

While large population is essential in conducting war, to a limited extent the mechanization of actual combat operations both on land and in the air has reduced the need for manpower. If this mechanization advances further in such fields as air transport, guided missiles and the like, it is conceivable that in future the large standing army may be reduced in size in view of the speed with which destruction may occur from strategic air bombing. A glimpse in this direction was afforded us in the latter part of the recent war :

> ". . . the perfect pattern of Air Force (is) completely integrated between reconnaissance, strategic and tactical bomb-

> ing, troop transport and airborne ground forces. With it, success crowned the Allied effort in the face of almost insuperable difficulty. There can be no question as to the decisive character of Air Force. It made possible the German onslaught in the beginnig and turned it back on the German homeland in the end. The Germans who had sought to fight another war on foreign soil, found themselves under direct assault and siege by air. Through the skill of their ground forces, they staved off defeat longer than their enemies had deemed possible. We must not lose sight of the fact that none of this could have been possible without Allied command of the sea and air over it."[4]

An overview of the material presented in this chapter indicates that the nations of the non-Communist world are strongly placed in their supplies of grain, particularly wheat, corn, oats and barley. They are also ahead of the Communist nations in the production of animal protein and fat foods, especially cattle, sheep and fish. They are well ahead in the sweet foods, both cane and beet sugar. For industrial materials, they have plentiful supplies of cotton, natural and synthetic rubber, wool, jute and timber. The Western nations and the Communist nations are about equally well provided with rice, swine and soyabeans. The non-Communist world produces relatively less tonnage of rye, millet, hemp and flax.

The conclusion is obvious : in basic foodstuffs and in other raw materials, the position of the Western nations is relatively strong as long as they are able to draw upon the supplies obtained from present allies or upon their own resources. It is apparent that any considerable shift in the alignment of national policies would automatically affect the economic position of the Western nations and their opponents. The decision of an important producing nation such as India to affiliate with one ideology or the other could have profound effects on the ability of either side to wage war successfully.

In further study in population and in area, non-Communist world is well ahead of the Communist world. How long this situation will prevail depends on the rapidity with which the Soviet Union succeeds in its attempt to dominate the nations of South-eastern and south-western Asia. Perhaps of greater importance than mere population figures is the character of the people. While not in itself a subject that the geo-strategist would normally consider, the effects of how well or poorly the people of a nation perform may have definite strategic results ; to this extent we cannot ignore human characteristics in relation to war.

The matter of geo-strategy's part in building a strong power, both economic and military, has been well stated by the geographer Jean Gottman : "The environment seems to provide the permanent material foundation both of nationalism, in so far as the nation is defined and affected by the territory it occupies, and of power, for the upbuilding of its status among other nations.... Power, after all, needs some basic resources and geography seems just the thing to give an appraisal of the potential."[5]

REFERENCES

1. *Recources for Freedom*, II, pp. 100, 103.
2. One cubic meter equals 0.2759 cord.
3. "American Raw-Material Deficiencies and Regional Dependence", Geographical Review 30 : 177-186, April, 1940.
4. Eugene E. Wilson, *Air Power for Peace*, McGraw-Hill Book Company, 1945, pp. 157-58.
5. "Geography and International Relations", in *World Politics* 3 : 153-173, January 1951. Quotation from page 154.

BASES OF NATIONAL POWER

MINERALS AND FUELS

Differing combinations of geo-strategic and geographic elements discussed earlier in this book account for wide variations in the economic and military strengths of the different nations, when combined with certain essentials that are not strictly geographic in nature. The geographic variables certainly include differing climates, the distribution of useful minerals, distribution of population and presence of certain raw materials. In addition to these, the single highly significant matter of geo-strategic location on the earth's surface is of paramount importance since this is the basic item underlying the distribution of climates, raw materials and population. Location on the earth in terms of latitude will determine the amount of effective solar energy that can be received at any given spot and this, in turn, governs in high degree the ability of that location to produce animal and vegetable foods, raw materials and other items necessarily essential if a nation is to develop an economy that will make it a powerful nation.

With sufficient land area, a favourable climate, plenty of timber, water, minerals fuels, metallic ores and water transport, a large and hard-working population may undertake to develop this complex of geographic factors, thus placing itself in a more favourable economic and military position than less favoured neighbours. Lacking one or two of the essentials, a nation pursues international trade in order to strengthen its economic structure and eventually its military forces. Though it may be unwise to place undue emphasis on economic sources of political strength, it is necessarily true that a strong and enduring political state cannot be based upon meagre or inadequate natural resources. After the debacle of 1944, Italy should be well aware of this fact.

POWER POTENTIALS

The inevitable distribution of the essentials for building economic and military strength leads to inequality of the war and peace potentials of the world's great powers. In view of the increased use of air power and the "shrinking" of distance in terms of time, it seems necessary to survey the strengths and weaknesses of the great powers in terms of their spheres of influence rather than in terms of the particular resources of each nation. On the basis of this concept, the following geographical associations seem reasonable in the light of present-day political thinking ; that is, the traditional geographic units of the decades before 1914 are these :

(1) Europe and North Africa
(2) United States and Canada
(3) Latin America
(4) South Africa and East Africa
(5) South-east Asia, including India and Pakistan ; East Indies, Australia
(6) West Asia
(7) Eastern Asia : China, Japan and Korea.

From the standpoint of present differences in ideology as well as economic interplay, a somewhat different alignment prevails :

(1) Western Europe and North Africa : United States, Canada, Australia, Japan and some Commonwealth countries.

(2) Latin America, excluding Argentina
(3) South Africa
(4) Soviet Union, China, Central and Eastern Europe
(5) West Asia, India and Pakistan.

Further refinement of the situation produces three principal groups :

(1) *Non-Communist World* : Western Europe and North Africa, United States, Canada, Australia, Japan, Latin America (except Argentina), Philippine Republic and few Commonwealth countries.
(2) *The Communist World* : Soviet Union, China, Central and Eastern Europe.
(3) Those parts of the world that are committed to neither the non-Communist world nor the Communist world but are too certain or too stable to depend upon them as sources of material for war : Argentina, South Africa, West Asia, India, Egypt and South-eastern Asia.

MINERAL RESOURCES

Warfare as it is conducted throughout most of the world at the present time is based essentially upon metals of different kinds ; therefore the distribution and control of mineral resources is a matter of extreme importance to any nation that is faced with the necessity for carrying on war activities. From the discussion that follows, it will be apparent that the non-Communist world is well endowed with most of the minerals that are needed to maintain military operations over a long period of time in spite of the enormous mineral potential of the Soviet Union and its allies. Because of rapid consumption of our best quality iron ore in the United States, their national position is less favourable than theretofore, but the development of new supplies in friendly nations seems not too difficult to accomplish. Otherwise they are in a very strong position, particularly if they can draw upon Canada for a large part of their needs in nickel, iron ore, and some other minerals. They have coal, molybdenum, aluminium and some other minerals in quantity but their rapid use of petroleum and their declining reserves of copper ore, lead and zinc, and rapidly advancing utilization of hydroelectric power indicate that they may have to develop new supplies in the near future and conserve more of those they now have. Their three principal mineral shortages seem to be manganese, chromite and tin and, of course, the development of radioactive materials makes urgent their need for more supplies of uranium and thorium. Though they do not have cobalt in any amount, they have been able to obtain it from Canada.

Assuming that non-Communist nations can work in reasonable harmony and that they are free to exchange minerals resources by peaceful trading methods, the outlook for meeting their peacetime and wartime mineral needs is, on the whole, very favourable. Material resources consisting of plentiful minerals as well as adequate food and materials for manufacture are essential if a nation is to maintain its favoured economic position in the present-day world. The mere presence of mineral resources alone, however, is not enough ; the minerals must be used wisely and economically by the citizens. To make the point clear, it is only necessary to suggest that the same natural resources were available for the use of the Indians that have served in the last many centuries to make India a leading military and economic nation. But the Indians made limited use of those resources before independence and it remained for the people of India to develop them to their highest point and to build a modern civilization based upon them. The largest amounts of physical resources do not necessarily result in the most advanced industrial civilization but their development must be undertaken by people who are capable of adapting them to the needs of both peace and war.

COAL AND IRON ORE

Until better or cheaper sources of power are available, the distribution of coal supplies throughout the world will remain inevitably important in any consideration of economic and military potentials. The world map of coal production indicates that coal is mined principally in the northern hemisphere, that is, in that part of the world where the most people live and where technological processes involving the use of coal are most advanced. The map, however, may be misleading because it does not indicate all the world's proved coal deposits. Within a given nation, the actual area of coal production may be very limited in extent ; for example, the distribution of coal and lignite fields in the United States and Canada is extensive but the largest production is concentrated in the Allegheny Plateau fields while many others remain relatively unexploited. Furthermore, many coal deposits are remote from populated places where the coal can be used most efficiently and coal is a commodity too expensive to transport long distances except in emergencies. It is best and most economically used near its place of origin and is useful even then only if geographical conditions favour its exploitation. From the standpoint of the distribution of coal supplies as a principal source of power, the United States and Canada seem to be in a highly favoured position.

A second look at the map, with reference to the *production* of coal, indicates that the United States surpasses any other single nation but since 1950 the increased production of coal in the Soviet Union and in East European countries now comes very near in amount to that production in the USA. In the long run, it is the amount of coal produced rather than the potential supply, that counts in developing an intensified industrial economy. The USA's potential supplies plus their actual production of coal are the most important present-day factors in maintaining their leading position in manufactured goods for both peace and war. In addition to these uses for power, coal is a most important mineral from which large supplies of chemical derivatives such as refrigerants, explosives and resins can be obtained ; in an advanced economy such as the USA's products are of inestimable usefulness and they would continue to need coal to produce them even though better sources of fuel might eventually be found.

The coal production of the eastern hemisphere is about equivalent to that of the western hemisphere, due partly to efforts of the Soviet Union to increase production. Production in the southern hemisphere is very little in spite of Australian reserves. The coal production in east and south-east-Asia is a good indicator of the general industrial development among Asiatic peoples especially India (except in Japan where coal is not too plentiful).

In heavy industries, necessary for manufacturing war goods, the production of coal and iron ore is closely related ; hence here is some correlation between amount of coal and amount of iron ore produced. In the western hemisphere and in Asia, the relationship is plain but in Europe, the situation is confused because many small nations are concerned with production of both commodities, some mining coal and its neighbour mining iron ore. Germany, for example, lacks sufficient iron ore to match its coal supplies ; France has barely enough coal to match her iron ore ; Britain is forced to import supplies of ore from North Africa, India and other places to keep her factories operating ; and several European nations rely on supplies of ore from Sweden and India. Since then, some iron ore developments have occurred in Labrador and Venezuela where mines of much promise are just beginning to come into commercial production. Since this ore is sufficiently available and valuable to meet Indian needs, the development promises to revise some of our major industrial centres.

"The real threat to national security lies in the fact that hostile action might seriously curtail the movement and production of ore. Deliveries to overseas countries could be halted by submarines (and, it might be added, by air attack). Six of the eight boats carrying ore from Chile were sunk and the other two withdrawn from service in the first week afte America entered World War II. The countries which are defficient in coal reserves, have to face hard days at the time of war ; with overseas supplies out off, ore would have to be drawn exclusively from sources within the continent."

PETROLEUM

As long as petroleum is the principal fuel used in aircraft, an understanding of the geography of petroleum is of vital importance to our national defence. Petroleum production is centred mainly on three continents : North America, Southwest Asia and the Soviet Union, and in the northern part of South America. Elsewhere in the world oil reserves are relatively small. In view of the urgent need for large supplies of petroleum, the anxiety on the part of Britain, the Soviet Union and other nations to develop fields in India and in West Asian countries and elsewhere is understandable and recent unstable political and economic situations in the West Asia reflect much manoeuvring for the most-favoured position on the part of those nations whose need for oil is greatest.

It will be noted that the United States' petroleum production constitutes more than half of the total for the entire world ; in other words, the USA is making use of its reserves at a fairly rapid rate. On the other hand, the actual production in relation to petroleum reserves in West Asia is low and, therefore, it would seem that the world's principal future supplies must come from that critical part of the world. Since petroleum can be transported with relative ease and cheapness, the geographical relationship between producing and consuming areas is of somewhat less importance that that of the commodities of greater bulk like coal or iron ore. As with coal the concentration of the world's petroleum production takes place chiefly in the northern hemisphere among the industrialized nations, except some valuable deposits in Venezuela.

HYDROELECTRICITY

Although generally less used than power produced from coal, water power is of great industrial importance when it can be converted into its most convenient form—hydroelectric power. It offers cleaner and more controlled heat than coal or petroleum and may be produced cheaply if geographical conditions are favourable. It should be noted, however, that hydroelectricity alone is of little value as a resource ; it must be combined with raw materials and labour if it is to function properly as a force. Africa, for example, with the greatest potential hydroelectric power on the globe uses this fuel less than any other inhabited area, since that continent is not well advanced industrially. It should be noted that hydroelectric power cannot be stored ; it must be used as it is produced. Further, to function as an efficient source of power, it must be produced in steady flow and volume. It can be used only short distances away from the place of production with the aid of transmission lines that normally are not more than 250 to 300 miles in length. Beyond that distance, the expenses of transmission are too great to justify the development of this form of power. It is fortunate that hydroelectric power can be utilized in any part of the world where other power resources are not present in quantity. In British Columbia, for example, sources of coal and petroleum are not plentiful but the mountainous land and the heavy precipitation evenly distributed throughout the year are favourable to the production of hydroelectric power.

STEEL ALLOYS

In the matter of coal, iron, petroleum and hydroelectricity, the United States and Canada are in favourable position in spite of a notable decline in United States iron ore reserves, offset to some extent by prospects for the development of Labrador and Venezuelan ores. In some other mineral resources, the USA is sufficiently well supplied to meet ordinary peacetime and military needs. As far as India is concerned, it has abundant supply of coal, iron, other metals and petroleum reserves and is able to meet threat in peace or war.

Tungsten : Of particular use in making steel for high speed cutting tools, ore of tungsten is in moderate supply in the USA coming mostly from mines in Nevada, California, Colorado and Idaho. Elsewhere the ores are widely distributed with eastern Asia, Portugal and Bolivia leading in production. Tungsten and molybdenum serve much the same purpose when used as ferro-alloys. It is estimated that between 85 and 90 per cent of the total world reserves are in China. Moreover, production costs in China are so low and the Chinese product is of such superior quality that the possibility of China's re-entry into the world market at any time is a powerful deterrent to large investment elsewhere in the world.

Nickel : Ore is abundant in Canada and her supply of this metal used in corrosion-resistant alloys is available for use in the USA, quantity coming from mines of the Sudbury district in Ontario. Lesser producing areas include New Caledonia in the South Pacific, Cuba and the Soviet Union.

Molybdenum. Fortunately the United States is well supplied with molybdenum, an excellent steel alloy. The USA has it in such quantity that they sometimes use it in place of some of the more scarce alloys in the manufacture of special steels. It produces more than nine-tenths of the world's output, mostly from a single mine in Colorado ; Chile produces a slight amount but no other country appears to have a large amount of the mineral. The USA does not foresee any serious shortage of this particular commodity.

Copper : Second only to iron ore in value, output and usefulness, copper ores are distributed widely throughout the world. This metallic ore has been mined for many centuries both for its own sake and for its use as an alloy with tin in the manufacture of bronze. The United States is by far the largest producer, supplying approximately one-third to one-half of the total world copper needs. Following in order of production are Chile, Canada, the Soviet Union, Northern Rhodesia, Congo and Japan. Copper is of special significance for the development of hydroelectricity since it is relatively cheap to produce and is an excellent conductor of electricity. Normally about half of the U.S. production is used for the transmission of electricity or in the manufacture of electrical products and machinery. Thus, copper is of special importance to those parts of the world in which hydroelectricity is used as a principal source of power when other fuels are lacking.

Zinc and Lead : Several other metals serve highly specialized purposes in manufacturing processes. Two in particular, lead and zinc, are not used in large quantity but nevertheless are of highly strategic significance. Up to the present time, the United States has been a leading producer of lead, supplying almost one-fourth of the world's needs and at the same time using a considerable amount of what she produces. Like copper, lead has been a metal of great usefulness for centuries of human existence. Common uses of the metal are found in storage batteries, high octane gasoline, protective coverings for radioactive minerals, paints, ammunition and similar products. Other parts of the world that are well supplied with lead include Australia, Mexico, Canada, the Soviet Union, Germany and Burma. Lead is used in such small quantities, however, that it need not be processed at the mine with the result that the United States, Germany and a few other countries normally smelt the ore at some distance from the place where it is obtained.

Zinc and lead ores are often found in the same locality and the United States generally produces about one-third of the world's zinc supply. It is also the largest consumer since this metal is an important galvanizing material and is one of the components in the manufacture of brass. It is used extensively in photography, the manufacture of paints and in a wide variety of other products. Canada, Germany, Australia, Mexico and the Soviet Union are other producers of importance.

Aluminium : Of more recent prominence than the other basic metals for industrial use, aluminium has been important only during the last half century. Its ore, bauxite, is distributed widely throughout the northern hemisphere and may be obtained without undue difficulty. The reduction of the ore, however, normally involves a large use of hydroelectricity in the process and for this reason, the extraction and other processing of the ore may occur a long distance from the source of supply. The United States produces more than one-third of the world's aluminium, with Canada, Germany and the Soviet Union following in that order. The metal is used in refining petroleum, cement making and in the manufacture of abrasives as well as for many other purposes including the transmission of electrical power. Though most of the processing of aluminium takes place in the northern hemisphere nations of the mid-latitudes, the production of bauxite in the lower latitudes of British Guiana, Surinam and Indonesia represents a considerable part of the world's supply of the raw material.

Vanadium : This fairly abundant metallic mineral is found widely distributed throughout the world, with principal producing area located in Germany, the United States, Peru and in the southern part of Africa. It produces a special-purpose metal somewhat approximating the qualities of nickel, chromium, molybdenum or manganese. It is used in the production of high quality resistant steels, and though it is not used in large quantity, it nevertheless serves a very definite purpose in certain types of commodities. The United States has adequate supplies to meet her needs in the manufacture of steel of great tensile strength and toughness. Vanadium steels are used in making extremely tough armour plate, automobile parts, gears, gun barrels and steel springs.

Uranium and Thorium : Since the advent of atomic weapons, the search for radioactive materials as sources of power has been enormously stimulated. The principal ore of uranium is pitchblende, from which the radioactive material is extracted. Exploration of the sources of uranium is still under way on a major scale, and thus far supplies have been found in some quantity in Canada, the United States, South Africa and East Africa as well as in a number of western European nations, India and Australia. Data on discoveries or production in the Soviet Union are incomplete or lacking and comparative figures of the production from other nations are not available since this is a highly strategic material. Another source of radioactive material is derived from thorium obtained from monazite. This ore is found in abundance on the western coast of the Deccan peninsula in India. Deposits are also known in Brazil and, to a limited extent, in the United States. The best available statistical material indicates that Brazil is the largest producer, followed by India and the federated Malay States. In the future, it is entirely possible that such rare substances as uranium and thorium will achieve greater prominence than minerals that are currently important.

Manganese : Manganese, of which the Soviet Union possesses almost half the world's supply, is found only in small quantities in the United States. It is highly essential as a strategic material for which no commercial substitutes have ever been found. It is a very important ingredient in the manufacture of certain types of steel, in the fabrication of dry batteries and in other commercial products. Almost all of the manganese used in the USA must be imported and since Russian supplies are not generally available, the USA depends upon imports from the Gold Coast and the Union of South Africa, India, Brazil, Chile and Cuba. The bulk of the manganese used in the United States goes into manufacture involving the removal of undesirable substances from steel. There is no apparent solution to the problem of shortage of this very important commodity in the USA except to depend upon other nations to supply them.

Chromite : The USA is deficient in supplies of chromite for the production of chromium, though it produces a small amount of the substance. This and manganese are ferro alloys of importance and are used as principal alloys of steel when extreme toughness is desired for such products as armour plate, stainless steel and steels that must endure high temperatures. It is particularly valuable in the manufacture of tools since they must be resistant to heat and corrosion. Chromite is regarded as an important strategic mineral and is found mainly in the Soviet Union, Zimbabwe, the Union of South Africa and Cuba . although many other parts of the world are able to produce small supplies. Normally the Soviet Union produces about one-fourth of the total amount used in the world. U.S. supplies of chromite must be imported and in recent years, it has obtained ore from Africa, Cuba, New Caledonia, the Philippines and Turkey.

Tin : The strategic mineral in which the USA is notably deficient is tin ore (cassiterite) which is produced mainly in Malay, Bolivia, Indonesia, the Congo and Nigeria although other south-eastern Asiatic nations have some supplies. This is the one mineral ore that is produced largely within a tropical environment and in part in the southern hemisphere. The Soviet Union, most of Western Europe, India, Canada and the United States are generally lacking in any large amounts of this material. There is no good substitute and it is used principally for plating other metals, particularly sheet iron that is, tin plate. It is a high-priced metal and with the exception of Malaya, it is usually processed some distance from the source of the ore. Outside of Malaya, tin smelting is concentrated in north-western Europe in the United Kingdom, the Netherlands,

Belgium and Germany. Some smelting is also done in China and Indonesia.

Titanium : Although the United States has small supplies of this metal, they are fortunate in that their neighbour Canada is able to provide them with some of their needs. Thus, though they are short of the material, the situation is not as critical as it is with manganese, chromite or tin. Titanium is a very light but strong metal of special usefulness in the manufacture of aircraft since its weight, strength and temperature characteristics are superior when used in structural parts.

In ordnance equipment, particularly of the airborne, hand-carried and mobile combat types, the use of titanium in place of steel would undoubtedly improve the combat efficiency of such equipment. The unsurpassed resistance of titanium to corrosion suggests numerous marine and chemical applications such as pipes and tubing ; condensers, plumbing fixtures, shafts, containers and laboratory equipment. In view of the many potential military applications for titanium and the strategic and tactical advantages that its use would afford, it is highly desirable that an intensive effort be made to develop large-scale, low-cost production as quickly as possible.

The situation of the nations of the non-Communist world with regard to the basic mineral resources upon which modern-day warfare is based seems moderately good on the whole. U.S. supplies of coal and iron ore are of good quality and they are reasonably accessible within the present limits of the non-Communist world. The main threat to their supply would appear to be the possibility of the insterruption of shipments because of attack on shipping by submarines or aircraft. Though not a critical matter as yet, the declining reserves of petroleum suggest that the non-Communist world may need to turn to nations outside the United States for much of its future supply. Electrical power is potentially available in large amounts yet to be developed and is not now a problem, though they might find some shortages under production stepped up for war objectives. Tungsten, nickel and copper are available to the non-Communist world within limits but shortages of supplies of lead and zinc are in prospect unless some conservation measures are undertaken. Aluminium is available in quantity, as well as vanadium and molybdenum. Increased use of radioactive materials will call for increased exploitation of uranium and thorium, of which the non-Communist world will be able to obtain reasonable amounts in so far as can be predicted on the basis of very recent exploration of sources. Manganese, chromite and tin remain their most critical shortage problems though supplies of chromite are obtainable from Turkey, and some sources for these metals are found scattered widely throughout the non-Communist nations.

With reference to future needs during the next quarter-century, the future production of copper, iron ore, (outside the United States), zinc and lead must double ; rubber production must increase by half and tin production must rise one-sixth if present military and economic standards of progress are to be maintained. We should be aware of our most critical needs and should take all necessary measures to place ourselves in a strong position in regard to mineral resources to carry on successful modern war.

CHAPTER SEVEN

AIR POWER

Air power is the sum-total of the entire war machinery of a country, which operates through the medium of air. The components, in addition to aircraft which is the basic platform for releasing all weapons, often referred to as a weapon itself, are the maintenance paraphernalia and the administration of all the requirements for the use of aircraft. Guided missiles are adjunct to offensive and defensive aircraft and therefore a part of the air power of a country. The total attacking and defending power through the air is thus air power and it is largely represented by the air forces. Largely because the modern armies and navies have their own private air forces which go under the names of army-air corps and fleet air arm respectively, these also form a part of air power.

Armies and navies have been fighting wars ever since the dawn of history but the third dimension was added to the realm of warfare only after the invention of aircraft when the potentialities of this formidable weapon were put to test.

Few years back, it was said that air power could be decisive in all future wars but the results of World War II proved that air power decidedly contributed a major share towards the victory. After World War II, the same came true in Arab-Israel war of 1967, in India-Pakistan war of 1971 and to an extent in Arab-Israel war of 1973.

"Modern air power has made the battle-field irrelevant" due to the fact that air power searches the enemy not only on the battle-field but right inside the safety and security of his homeland. It is capable of hitting him where it hurts the most. It gets the results fastest. Having started as an adjunct to land and sea warfare, air power emerged into its own as an independent arm only after the effectiveness was tried out during war. No wonder Sir Winston Churchill made the following statement in 1949 ; "For good or ill, air mastery today is the supreme expression of military power and fleets and armies, however necessary, must accept a subordinate rank." It is unfortunate that military thinkers like Fuller could never get used to this kind of modernistic outlook for the reason that they could not mentally divorce army doctrines from the warfare. The basic war for them existed on the surface where armies fought opposite each other. The idea of a change of dimension to an extent by submarine and fully by aircraft was hard to conceive for them. If at all they tried to project themselves, they could, at the most, think of aircraft with short range and limited capability, just enough to help the army in its battles ; no wonder they looked at aircraft as a long range weapon of army or navy. Various wars in recent times have proved the converse of this. Battles can be fought decisively by aircraft and armies and navies are required to go and occupy the land or island, even that could be done by dropping through air by means of parachute or transported by helicopters. Does not that open an entirely new dimension to the problem ? It does because it brings before the vision, a certain possibility which cannot be brushed aside—supremacy of air power.

Having placed air power in its proper place through an objective study, we may proceed to explore it further. 'Air power is not divisible.' This statement means that it should not be judged by emphasis on any particular aspect of air power but on totality, just as war, in the truest sense, is not divisible *e.g.*, army's war, naval war or air war, all the three powers will have to be used in order to achieve the desired end—the enemy's defeat ; their employment, however, will be guided by the circumstances governing the war, geographical, tactical and strategical, in an overall end pointed by the aims. The three powers are only three means to achieve the same final goal. Similarly the various parts which form air power are means towards achievement of the aim set out before air power. As the aim of war cannot be divided into separate aims of air power, land power and sea power, in the same fashion the aim of air power cannot be divided into smaller aims of each part of air power. The totality of aim makes it indivisible or, in other words, incapable of being reduced to smaller aims. At the same time, various objectives could be nominated separately, making the sum total of all such objectives as the final indivisible aim - victory in war.

The factors which condition the effectiveness of air power are :

(*a*) Aircraft ; (*b*) Aircrews ; (*c*) Weather ; (*d*) Intelligence ; (*e*) Planning and administration ; (*f*) Maintenance ; (*g*) Weapon system ; and (*h*) Equipment required.

Flexibility and surprise are the inherent principles of war in air power. An aircraft operating from the same base can attack many a diverse targets ; alternatively, many aircraft operating from various bases can attack the same target. A fast moving aircraft flying low gives hardly any warning of its arrival. In terms of long range aerial attacks, there is economy of effort because one aircraft could achieve, under certain conditions, as much as a full brigade or a flotilla of ships. In terms of concentration of force, again, aircraft can, by passing the war fronts, achieve as much as they did in Rhur Valley in Germany during the thousand bomber raids. But the offensive action of aircraft is perhaps the maximum attainment of this principle of war. Let alone offensive role of bombers, ground attack and assault aircraft, even when engaged in defensive role, air power will have offensive action as its methods. Almost at no time an aircraft is supposed to be on defensive action ; it is invariably either offensive action or evasive action. Defensive action in terms of army or navy would only mean passive wait for aircraft to be destroyed.

If war is defined to impose the will of a country over the opponent, then the elements of this imposition are will-power or moral courage of a nation, augmented by its resources and fighting capability. For reasons emanating from the study of history, it can be clearly discerned that air power has a major contribution towards moral courage of a nation. It gives the psychological strength from the fact that it is spectacular. Imagine one single aircraft flying low just above a bridge marching past or a couple of destroyers cruising along. The dimensional difference accentuates attention psychologically. Whereas it raises the morale of a nation, it puts the enemy on defensive at the same time by keeping him guessing as to where precisely the attack is going to be. Dimension, therefore, is the basic factor which makes air power different from land and sea power. To judge air power by the same yardstick as navy or army would therefore be incorrect if the initial handicap in favour of or against dimension was not applied. Judging is accepted between the similar and not divergent kinds. Air power is different from land or sea power and hence the question of comparison does not arise. It has a place and pedestal of its own. The only common thing it has with sea or land power is aim and air power has surpassed them both in achievement of the same, in proportionate summation of the results of all the wars fought after its maturity. Churchill's saying in 1949, quoted above, stands true.

Various fields or roles in which air power operates are :

(*a*) Offensive role, also referred to as strategic or bomber role.

(*b*) Defensive role or air defence.

(*c*) Tactical role or the role in support of army, also referred to as offensive air support.

(*d*) Maritime reconnaissance and maritime strike role or the role in support of navy.

(*e*) Transport role comprising strategic, tactical and battlefield transportation of army and navy, in addition to paratroopers, assault forces, casualty evacuation, communication of VIPs and Commanders, special clandestine operations and aid to psychological warfare.

(*f*) Air reconnaissance or gathering intelligence through

aerial means, tactical or strategical, for the use of all the services. Also, aerial survey role for mapping.

The role of air power in World War II brought out certain conclusions as broad guidelines, emanating from experience, which were formulated for and brought before those interested in the study of air power. History keeps on bringing out new lessons. The wars fought after World War II indicate that the emotions which used to cry out "totality" of war were subdued. In other words, people realized that total wars were suicidal, hence the wars subsequently fought, whatever the extent of enmity, were localized in nature—nowhere the slogan was total or unconditional surrender—the aims were limited in each case, and where the aims were confused, the wars were prolonged like the one in Vietnam.

The clear-cut definition of aims on the part of those fighting war, through declaration or through action, therefore, is one big advancement after World War II. Localization of aims or objectives, *i.e.*, limiting them to geographical, regional or to certain conditions which prevent them from becoming all-encompassing, has resulted from this. Futility of total war and vast horrors, of which most understanding people are aware, is almost established, more so with the generation which has been a witness to widespread devastation during World War II.

World has still not arrived at a stage through evolution where reason may be the deciding factor for disputes or differences of opinion. Even the UN seems a machinery without legs, sometimes being twisted and pressurized by the interested parties without much reference to reason. Might, still, remains the resort for settlement of disputes. However, the application, in terms of methods, has undergone change. It is no more the primitive concept resting entirely on the armed strength. It is now the scientific application of using resources economically for obtaining the limited aims, not for total destruction of the enemy. This is where war has become civilized and this is where the application of sophisticated weapons becomes most important aspect of fighting a war. Aircraft is the most sophisticated weapon which today's generation has for fighting a war. The lightning attacks by the Israeli planes in 1967, Mirage and Mystere, on Arab airfields, precisely timed, provided a fine example of decisiveness of air power. This is what Winston Churchill's son and grandson, Randolph S. and Winston S. have to say in *The Six Day War* :

"This was one of the swiftest and most decisive victories the world has ever seen. In less than four days, the Israelis had broken Egypt's proud army of 100,000. Thousands of vehicles had been taken or destroyed, together with more than 700 Russian-made tanks, some of them the most modern in the world. Their victory was due largely to the supeior quantity of their manpower. In particular of their officers, also to the fact that they know what they were fighting for—the existence of their country and the lives of their women and children. Their ruthless determination, their flexibility, their speed of decision and manoeuvre, coupled with superior training, was decisive. But such a rapid and dramatic result could never have been achieved but for the total air supremacy achieved by the Israeli Air Force throughout the skies of the Middle East".

In the words of General Hod, the Israeli Air Force Commander, "We hacked them continuously, we did not make the mistake we made in 56."

The Indian Air Force, in the 1971 war, had established similar air supremacy in Bangladesh and the fall of Dacca was due entirely to the dramatic air attacks. That the decisive element was imposed by the Air Force in surrender of Pakistani forces in Bangladesh, is abundantly clear from the facts. The speed with which the air battle moves towards decisiveness is a condition rarely attained by armies and navies.

AIR SUPERIORITY

The Concept of air superiority as a condition in which own forces may operate without interference by the enemy aircraft, was evolved to maturity during World War II. Air superiority was further divided into general or local. General air superiority or air supremacy is possible only when the entire combat air force of the enemy could be neutralized, *i.e.*, destroyed, damaged or incapacitated to operate by crippling the essentials on which the air force operates, *i.e.*, aircraft, runways, servicing facilities, refuelling facilities, radar stations for the interceptors. Runways can be repaired within hours, servicing facilities and refuelling facilities being diversified are difficult to destroy completely, damaged radar stations can be repaired soon, destroyed ones can be replaced in days. Aircraft on ground are, therefore, about the finest 'target' but they are not always easy to destroy in view of their dispersal in well constructed blast pens. Aerial combat has an element of chance and surprise, hence it cannot be decisive if the enemy has aircraft of commensurate performance and well trained air crews. The sum total of all this is that complete air superiority or air supremacy is almost a redundant idea when fighting with an equally prepared enemy. Local air superiority, however, is a desirable condition for favourable results. Local air superiority, however, is fleeting in nature ; it exists for a limited time in a limited area and vanishes as soon as there is enemy air intervention.

STRATEGY AND TACTICS

Strategy has been defined as artifice or finesse which gives a decided advantage over the enemy whereas tactics are the science or art of manoeuvring in presence of the enemy. From the definition, it emanates that sound strategy gives the long-term advantage whereas sound tactics give immediate advantage while fighting against the enemy. Strategy aims at a distance in time or space, ultimately helping in achievement of aims whereas tactics concern with day-to-day fighting on the front.

In terms of air power, strategy, therefore, aims at long-term objectives which may not have immediate concern with fighting at the front but the ultimate. Let us take an example to make the issue clear. If we could destroy the industry which feeds the enemy's war effort, it is natural that the enemy will not be able to sustain the war for a long time to come ; alternatively, if we destroy the enemy's fuel reserves, it will have a similar effect on his capacity to fight or if we may destroy his aeroplane factories, he will not be able to put up air opposition in time to come. It is this part of the aerial warfare which is most important. The strategic aim of air power is to destroy all those resources on which the enemy's war capability depends in the long run and this is achieved through bomber. The method, no doubt, has to be offensive as the attacks have to be carried out in the enemy's safe places or strongholds, away from the front line, deep into his territory in well protected areas. This major part of aerial warfare is termed strategic offensive or bomber offensive and this constitutes the most effective role of the air power.

The tactics, in terms of aerial warfare, are the participation in the army battle, being fought on the ground at or near the front, against the enemy army in order to support own army by neutralizing enemy targets which are normally beyond the organic weapons of own army. The tactics concern air power in fighting the army battle for the army and the naval battle for the navy. It involves participation in the actual war front while operating from the air.

Apart from the above generalization, each strategic move has its own tactics. Tactics, for that matter, are there for each operation whether the operation is aimed at long-term advantage or short-term advantage. There are tactics for each role of the air power. In this sense, tactics mean even the height, route, speed, attack pattern, evasion pattern and the selection of weapons, *i.e.*, bombs, rockets, missiles or guns suited to the objectives to be taken.

Strategy aims at ultimate whereas tactics aim at immediate end. The Allies bomber attacks on Germany were strategical in nature while the role of the RAF in the desert warfare, in support of Monty's army, was tactical. The Indian bomber attacks on the Karachi fuel dump, Changa Manga fuel dump and the airfields at Manipur, Sargodha, Multan, Murid and other airfields in 1971 were strategic raids while the Indian air power operated in Bangladesh in a tactical role in order to facilitate the liberation forces. The aim was to prevent the Pakistan Air Force as an opposing force to operate so that our forces could operate freely.

In case of future limited wars, however, the difference between strategy and tactics is likely to be narrowed down as the war itself would assume a highly speedy disposal with simultaneous or synchronized attacks on the short-term as well long-term objectives, reducing the possibilities of prolonged wars and thereby determining victory or defeat in the quickest possible time. As strategy aims at long-term or ultimate advantages, what would be termed as strategy when there is no long-term or ultimate ? When the entire war is aimed at the immediate, what is strategic ? Obviously we do not want to start hair splitting and insist that within the immediate also there is relative immediate and the relative ulimate. In order to conclude the subject, therefore, we generalize again by stating that in future wars, tactics will merge with strategy in aerial warfare in view of the fact that the aerial warfare will aim at quick decisiveness right from the word 'go'. In order to achieve such quick results, however, it is necessary that the quantum of air power should be sufficiently large and its quality be first rate.

Strategy for developing countries, in matter of air power, can therefore be evolved in the light of experience gained during the wars fought without interference of super-powers, in which the long-term objectives become short term as a lesson.

Strategy has another connotation also. The foreign policy of a country defines who the friend is and who is the potential enemy. The policy makers are continuously busy sorting out problems in the external sphere of a country's relations. They sort out most things through negotiations and yet with some countries, it becomes impossible to negotiate in keeping with self-respect and self-interest of the country. It is only such countries which become potential enemies. Once a country is known to be a potential enemy, all defence preparation has to be geared to match the strength of such a country. It is also in self-interest to keep warding off the threat of war up to a time that it is possible to take on an armed conflict. For countries which are basically neutral and friendly like ours and which want to settle all differences through peaceful means, not in view of weakness but because of wisdom, it does sometimes become necessary to fight a war.

After the repression in Bangladesh started on March 25, 1971, India took the side of the oppressed and did her best to arrive at an amicable solution of the problem, first by appealing to Pakistan and later to the world opinion but strangely no one cared to listen. India gave whatever support she could and sympathy to Bangladesh, following the correct path but the then rulers of Pakistan thought they knew how to deal with India : they started intruding the Indian air space (and provoking India so that IAF had to shoot down three PAF Sabre jets.) Pakistan got provoked and launched a pre-emptive attack on seven Indian airfields on December 3, 1971. This started the full-fledged war. The war was inevitable under these circumstances, however, as the coming events had cast their shadow. India was prepared for this. This is the kind of war which could not have been avoided. In other words, this war had to be fought. The war, incidentally, was started by aerial action and it came to an end with a final aerial stroke on Dacca. In between, too, all major decisive victories were determined by the air power.

The above was a correct example of defence policy following the foreign policy. The Chinese invasion of 1962, however, was a different story. At that time the foreign policy, for some reason, did not dictate the defence policy. In other words, the defence was neither ready nor planned for, for the Chinese threat, as a result when the brunt came it, could not be faced ; preparation or planning, it may be appreciated, is the first requirement of defence and it can never be done unless the threat is defined because all preparation has to be commensurate to the threat expected. The man who hopes a burglar to come at night, may keep a pistol handy—he does not think in terms of an anti-aircraft gun being hidden under his pillow. Now, supposing an aircraft comes and strafes his bed at night, surely, he is not prepared for it. His assessment of the threat has gone wrong.

The second war with Pakistan in 1965 was a clear-cut case of an ambitious neighbour trying to invade India. After Ayub was well settled in the one-man chair of Pakistan, he thought he was powerful enough to grab Kashmir, so he sent the infiltrators there, followed by regular troops. Being a close neighbour India had come to know the plan of Ayub, perhaps through captured infiltrators, and hence was ready to meet the challenge. Ayub had told his people that marching right up to Delhi was no problem for his forces. The battles that ensued at Chhamb-Jaurian as well as Khem Karan made him realize that it was not so. The Indian Army, supported by the Indian Air Force, started the diversionary front by advancing towards Lahore, right up to Ichhogil canal. This was augmented by Canberra and fighter raids on Pakistan airfields, pounding them regularly. These two actions brought balance in Pakistan's thinking. After the ceasefire, however, both the parties went back to their original positions, unfighting the war which had been fought. The war of 1965 was another example of the defence policy following the foreign policy. As mentioned earlier, this had started after the sad event in 1962.

Having once assessed the threat and scope of the same, during peace time, it becomes necessary to evaluate it or weigh it so as to take the essence. The preparation in terms of air power follows next. As often believed by many people, the weighing is not done by having more number of aircraft than the enemy has in each category but by assessing own needs. These needs are the strategic needs and governed by (*a*) geography of the enemy country, taking farthest areas into consideration in which the enemy's vital points and vital areas are situated, (*b*) radius of action of own bombers and fighters in relation to distance of enemy' vital areas and vital points, (*c*) defensive preparedness of the enemy to fight when you go to attack, and (*d*) offensive capabilites of the enemy to attack.

Now, in order to have a correct assessment of enemy's offensive and defensive capabilities as well as the information of his vital areas and vital points which should make the list of own targets, it is necessary to have reliable sources of intelligence. Having seen that intelligence is the basis from which all planning for strategy springs, it is of vital importance that any country who wants to plan correctly, must have the foolproof system of intelligence, specialized in collecting and collating the latest essential data, on the intention of the potential enemy as well his defence preparedness. Without meeting this requirement, all planning is futile. The essence of dependable intelligence is that it must not be vague or lengthy hinting at many possibilities—newspapers coming from other countries can serve this purpose. Precision should be the essence of all intelligence—blacks and whites, no doubtful greys. Having overcome the first stage in strategic planning, the next should be the planning of own forces, *i.e.*, requirement in number and type of each category of aircraft, calculated through a worked out system related to the number of enemy targets, on the basis of force required to destroy each target. The defensive and transporting forces must then be worked out on derivative requirements from the summation of the enemy's offensive forces and own requirements in terms of total defence resources respectively.

The forces that worked out, no doubt, may be much more than the country's economy permits, hence prudence as a factor must be introduced in the strategic planning. For instance, if there are three countries who are likely to be potential enemies, it is necessary not to fight with all three of them together. One at a time, that too when it is a must, should be the principle. How does one go around making sure that one should not fight with more than one enemy at a time ? This is where diplomacy takes over, Chankaya as well as Mechiavelli ; and that is where this is about to go out of our context.

In yet another sense, the strategy of aerial warfare exists basically in the air power's own agents, the basic and the secondary. The basic agent of air power is a bomber and its strategy offensive, emanating from the saying that if war has to be fought, offensive is the best from the defensive. The secondary agent, the defensive, deals with the weapons of air defence, one out of them is interceptor aircraft. As the tactical and maritime reconnaissance roles are there to aid army and navy although offensive in action, they follow the strategy of army and navy respectively, which these days, as in the days of old, can either be offensive or defensive, depending on various conditions dictating the situation. Air Recce role is, again, offensive, particularly the Strat Recce which continuously works during peace and war contributing its bit to the ultimate aim.

Strategy followed by transport and logistics role is guided by a combination of factors. In a country like ours, this arm keeps on building stocks for the army by supply dropping in the difficult far-flung areas in peace, almost at the wartime schedules. The inadequacy of the roads in the hilly areas dictates the objectives of transport arm in peacetime. In wartime, the strategy guiding this arm can be very offensive under conditions of limited protection, as was achieved during the Indo-Pak war of 1971. Transport played offensive role in the Eastern Sector through launching paratroopers and in the Western Sector by dropping loads of bombs successfully on the enemy targets—there is hardly any better example of flexibility than this. In its pure role, air transport, however, is irreplaceable.

CHAPTER EIGHT

NAVAL AIR SURVEILLANCE

It would be difficult to conceive a situation in which the inherent nature of the struggle between air power and sea power would stand out in more striking relief than in the conflict which began in the autumn of 1939, Great Britain was far weaker than Germany in the air and substantially superior in warship strength. Most of the British bases were within the range of German bombers, particularly after the German conquests of 1940, while a British blockade against Germany was being maintained on the broad sea.

The same would have been true, however, although in somewhat lesser degree, even if Great Britain had enjoyed parity or superiority in the air, for the defence of shipping was in any case a problem for Britain but not for Germany. Germany's naval inferiority precluded her attempting to maintain a shipping of her own, except in the Baltic and along the Norwegian coast. Whatever evidence the war was to bring forth, it was thus clear at the outset that Britain's ability to retain her seaborne communications and to sever those of her enemy was initially established by superior sea power.

The first brush between the German air arm and the British Fleet since the World War, and one of a far larger scope than ever occurred in that war, took place on September 26, 1939. The Germans immediately claimed substantial success but the next day Winston Churchill, then First Lord of the Admiralty, read in the House of Commons the wireless communication he had just received from the Commander-in-Chief of the Home Fleet : "Yesterday afternoon," the message read, "in the middle of the North Sea, a squadron of British capital ships together with an aircraft carrier, cruisers and destroyers was attacked by about 20 German aircraft. No British ship was hit and no British casualties were incurred. One German flying boat was shot down and another is reported to be badly damaged."

The results of this bout were representative of several that followed. By April 11, 1940, there had been five raids on Scapa Flow, yet according to the results announced to the House of Commons—and the House, it must be observed, is extraordinarily jealous of the truth in declarations of this nature—there had been only one minor injury to a cruiser which had been repaired in a few weeks.

"The enemy", Churchill declared, "has shown himself increasingly gun-shy in his attacks on Scapa and this is hardly to be wondered at, since the batteries, especially when reinforced by the powerful batteries of the Fleet, can deliver what is probably far the heaviest concentration of anti-aircraft fire in the world." In the raid of the previous evening (April 10), Churchill revealed that 60 planes had taken part without doing the slightest damage, although six of their number had been shot down.

Two days before, on April 9, a similar battle had taken place at sea. The British Fleet in the North Sea at about the level of Bergen was "attacked continuously" during the afternoon by German aircraft. Churchill asserted that the only damage done was to two cruisers that had been "slightly injured by splinters which, however, did not necessitate even temporary removal from the Fleet." One "very heavy bomb" hit the Rodney but her deck armour resisted the impact. The vessel has not been damaged but 10 men had been injured.

These were clear-cut victories for the surface fleets. But when Churchill made these announcements, the campaign in Norway had already begun and in this campaign, the German air fleets were to win their first great victory over the British surface fleet—a victory not measured in terms of vessels sunk or aircraft downed, for the battle in which such destruction might have occurred never took place.

In order to win the decision in Norway, the British would have had to maintain a standing patrol of warships in the Skagerrak. Because of the nearness of the main German naval base with its several powerful vessels, not merely destroyer squadrons but important forces would have been necessary. But this was on the very shores of German-occupied Denmark, where huge bomber squadrons established themselves with astonishing rapidity at the beginning of the campaign. The British Admiralty decided that if they attempted to maintain a constant patrol in the Skagerrak, "the losses which would be inflicted upon that patrol from the air would, undoubtedly, very soon constitute a naval disaster."

Even raids in force into the Skagerrak would have been useless, especially with the lengthening days of that time of year, for the German reconnaissance planes would spot such a force long before it arrived, and the British would find awaiting them not German transports but the great bombing formations of the Luftwaffe. The British therefore had to content themselves with a submarine blockade, a blockade which could not have been decisive in halting the German invasion in any case and which was rendered even less effective by the constant German air patrols.

This was bitter medicine for Britain to swallow. Churchill now expressed his view of the air threat in quite different terms from those he had so recently used. "It is no use thinking of this war in terms of the last war," he declared, "The power of the air has greatly affected—some believe it has decisively affected—the movements of fleets and armies. We must not exaggerate this new factor—I find myself almost resenting the exaggeration of this new factor—but neither must we refuse to give it its deadly due."

The events of the following 20 months demonstrated all too clearly the terrible content of that "deadly due." Not all of those events were to the disadvantage of Britain and her Allies—the brilliant sword stroke of Taranto furnished the first victory of aircraft over the mightiest ships of the line but in the main the successes of airplanes against surface ship could not but strike at the security of those nations which relied chiefly upon sea power in traditional form. The sinking in January 1941 of the cruiser Southampton in the Sicilian Strait and the heavy damage inflicted upon the aircraft-carrier illustrious in the same action were auguries of evil things to come. The damages suffered at Crete in May of the same year were far more serious and before the year 1941 was out, the terrific aerial blows struck by Japan in the Pacific sounded what seemed like the death knell not merely of an era but of that whole span of recorded time in which surface ships of war had ruled the seas.

Especially after that black week in December 1941 when four capital ships were sunk or capsized and six others badly disabled as a result of attack from the air, the terrible swift lance of the attack airplane swept all before it in the popular imagination. The prophets of the new order were not slow in raising their trumpets. Soon there was issuing from the press and radio a flood of proclamations to the effect that all ships save those which flew were practically useless, and that battle-ship, particularly, were merely death traps for their crews, deserving only to be retired to museums along with the blunder-buss and other outlived weapons of war. Later the battles of the Coral Sea and the Midway Islands served only to confirm what to many had become the obvious.

A great change had indeed fallen over the aspect of war at sea. The advent of the attack airplane was at least as revolutionary as anything which had occurred since the introduction of steam on the warship. It was clear that not only the tactics but also the whole strategy of naval warfare had been thrown off their foundations and that, whatever new re-adjustments were made, the situation would never again be as it was. The airplane was bound to remain an instrument which would command first attention in any naval battle or campaign of the future.

On the other hand, the opinion that the ascendancy of air-craft over ships had been completely demonstrated, was not only premature but was based on a careless or biased reading of the available facts. Britain, throughout the period of her terrible inferiority in air power, had retained effective command of the vital Atlantic. That was the basic fact in comparison with which all others were secondary. Not only did her warships ply that sea with little hindrance but by the autumn of 1941 she had also reduced to insignificant figures, her shipping had bearded Mussolini with impudence and for a long time almost with impunity, losing not a single capital ship to air attack in all its many peregrinations through those waters. When the German Air Force finally moved in, the situation had become much tighter but still British warships hurried about the Middle Sea and still none of their meagre store of capital ships was lost to air attack. When the Southampton was finally sent down, the first British warship of cruiser size to be lost to air attack in more than a year of war, Lord Chatfield was led to exclaim : "Who would have dreamed that this was all, the German Air Force could have accomplished with their innumerable opportunities."

The situation changed after that event. The skies grew ever darker over the water-borne vessel and in the rising storm of bombs and torpedoes dropped from the air, more and more ships went to their death. Yet still the surviving warships, and their number always remained far greater than those which had been sunk, ruled the broad reaches of the sea. The disaster which overtook eight American battleships in a single morning obscured the real significance of that blow. The Japanese had not struck at our Fleet in order to achieve dominance in the air, for such a result could not possibly follow. They did it to gain for their own battle fleet an unchallengeable ascendancy in the Pacific. And behind the shield of their then unmatched sea power, their water-borne invasion forces spread apace, snatching one island realm after another in dismal sequence.

Nevertheless, it was clear that the warship must find some way of defending itself adequately from the skies or its day was done. Pearl Harbour had proved nothing. That a number of battleships at anchor, unready for action and gunnery stations mostly unmanned, should fall victim to the torpedoes of an unopposed sneak attack argued nothing from which tactical lessons might be drawn. The radar warning of the approach had not been heeded. If it had been, the story would have been vastly different. On the other hand, the destruction of the Prince of Wales and Repulse in the China Sea was a wholly different matter. These fast, powerfully armed and heavily armoured warships had been, in the words of their own admiral, "looking for trouble." They found it in the air and had perished under it. And down with them went their 16 big guns without having fired a shot. If such vessels could be so easily despatched, what types could hope to survive ?

Many lessons were read at that time into the sinking of those two great ships off Malaya, but the most fundamental one was almost completely ignored. And that fundamental fact was simply that the Prince of Wales and Repulse were not abreast of the needs of the time for anti-aircraft defence. The event did not prove the obsoleteness of the capital ship type, nor did it prove that such ships could not operate except with air fighter escort. It proved only that those ships, armed as they were on that day, were not equal to defending themselves against attack by any substantial number of aircraft.

There are several ways in which a ship can defend itself against air attack, though all of them have their peculiar limitations. It may, if it is big enough, provide itself with a massive structural defence, the so-called "passive" resistance offered by heavy armour and compartmentation. But only the largest combatant types, not including aircraft carriers, can avail themselves of anything like adequate protection from vital damage by heavy aerial bombs. And armour does not protect against extensive superficial damage. Nor can it, important as it is, guarantee completely the life of the ship as the loss of the Prince of Wales clearly proved.

A defence which is, however, available to every type of vessel, large or small, combatant or unarmed, is simple evasion by rapid manoeuvring. Provided it has plenty of sea room and is under way, a vessel can make itself an extraordinarily difficult target for high-flying bombing craft. The bomb, being propelled only by the force of gravity, takes a relatively long time to descend and the plane must itself reach a particular point in space before it can release the bomb with any hope of hitting. The actual bomb release is usually observed from the target vessel and no bomb sight, however ingenious, can anticipate the moves, the ship will make after the bombs have been dropped. A particularly speedy vessel can often elude even the missiles of dive-bombers and torpedo planes and the latter must in any event expose themselves to multiple dangers which high-flying planes can largely avoid. And the limited bomb or torpedo load of the plane precludes any large number of successive tries.

"Evasive action" is always used by ships under way, whatever other defences are available. It explains to a large degree why a much greater number of ships have weathered air attacks successfully than have perished under it. During the early days of World War II, the British relied very heavily on movement to keep their priceless warships afloat. Battleships averaged 25 days of each month at sea, a record that would have been incredible in World War I. During the Norwegian campaign of April 1940, British warships venturing into the fjords maintained a constant, almost fantastic, motion. Destroyers carried out repairs and took on oil from attending tankers while under way. At the cost of heavy consumption of fuel, excessive wear on machinery and extraordinarily trying exactions upon personnel. British ships remained afloat during those critical days when more adequate defences were being developed.

But obviously, any defensive measure which does not destroy planes, must be supplemented by others. The enemy may be forced to make more sorties and drop more bombs but he will eventually get hit. And one hit pays for many misses. The area round one's ship must also be made dangerous to hostile planes.

Now it happens that of all fighting craft which go to sea, the airplane is by far the most fragile. The supreme importance of weight precludes any substantial burden of protection. Most military planes today are "armoured" but the armour is of thin gauge, sufficient only against light machine-gun bullets, and is confined to a few portions of the craft. The complete structural interdependence of the various parts adds to the vulnerability of the whole. The result is that an explosive shell of small calibre and even machine-gun bullets, may destroy it with direct hits and a medium calibre shell can frequently destroy it if it bursts in the near vicinity. One frequently reads of planes which have returned to their bases despite severe damage from enemy fire, but against such accounts must be weighed the colossal score month by month of planes downed or destroyed on the ground on all the fighting fronts. The airplane is thus a military anomaly in that it can hurl the most elephantine of projectiles and yet be mortally stung by a pebble.

The fact that the airplane can be defeated by small missiles is its vital tactical weakness. For small-calibre guns can easily be borne aloft in other aircraft and be plentifully distributed along the decks and superstructure of water-borne vessels. Defence of the kind that kills, is thus provided either by one's fighter planes or by anti-aircraft fire.

In this kind of active, hitting defence, the fighter plane has several pronounced advantages. Since it can bring its guns close to the target, it fires at point blank range usually on a course in line with the enemy's ; and its gunnery problems are hence exceedingly simple. It can meet the enemy at any altitude and, above all, it can go out to meet him not only long before he comes within range of anti-aircraft guns but also before he approaches his offensive goal. Often it will destroy him on or over his own bases. These facts have been of such importance that the public was easily persuaded by certain extremists to believe that only airplanes can defeat airplanes. As applied to the naval picture, the argument ran that warships were helpless for offensive missions unless covered by an "umbrella" of aircraft.

The only trouble with that argument is that umbrellas of aircraft are, by no means, easy to provide over a fleet at sea. Land-based fighters cannot be relied upon to be present when needed, even in coastal areas. The attack of enemy aircraft is so swift in developing and comes to so quick a consummation that it is useless to call upon planes which are not already with the fleet. And the very limited endurance in terms of flight time of the usual fighter plane precludes any constant patrol over the sea save under extraordinary circumstances as, for example, when the Germans sent the Gneisenau and Scharnhorst on their famous dash through the Channel in February 1941.

An operation of such limited time and purpose could be amply provided for by large relays of fighter planes which for the moment could be spared from other duties. But the British in their constant operations in the Mediterranean could not afford any such extravagance.

When one considers fleets operating far out at sea, the value of the land-based fighter as a defence falls to zero. It is not simply a question of range, but of ability to keep the sea. The extreme cruising radius of the plane, which is limited enough in fighter types, must be divided by its high cruising speed ; and the result gives the number of hours which the craft can spend in the air. Subtract from that the time spent in flying to and from the fleet to be protected, the reserve of flight endurance necessary for emergencies and the potential flight time lost when the engines are opened wide for combat, and the remainder becomes painfully lean, vanishing completely beyond a certain narrow margin of coastal waters.

The aircraft carrier is the obvious answer. The carrier is the only means of providing fighter-plane defence for a fleet far out at sea. But the carrier is a large and expensive vessel and considering the investment in resources that goes into it, the number of planes it can operate is not great. Besides, the admiral who has one or two aircraft carriers under his command, is rightly unwilling to restrict it to a purely defensive role. The result is that the majority of the planes carried will be attack planes and during action, most of the fighters will be sent out offensively as a cover for those planes. There then remains on hand a bare handful of fighter planes for the defence chiefly of the carrier itself, which, because of its inherent vulnerability and its lure for enemy aircraft, becomes a burden upon rather than an aid to the entire force. In more than one instance during the Pacific war of 1942-43, an aircraft carrier has been saved from destruction by the fire of the very vessels whose defence it was her original function to serve. And in any case, the number of aircraft carriers in existence at any one time has thus far been exceedingly small, far smaller than the number of any other type of combatant ship. Thus, to insist upon warships having fighter protection before venturing into combat areas would be to impose an intolerable restriction upon their offensive potentialities.

The defence of the ship of war from air attack ultimately and chiefly devolves upon her own anti-aircraft fire. Unfortunately, the story of the development of naval anti-aircraft fire during World War II, is one which for reasons of security cannot be told in any of its significant details. But when it is told, it will be a story of fantastic ingenuity and accomplishment. It will be a story of one of the two or three outstanding tactical revolutions of the war. For the difference in anti-aircraft power between the battleship of Pearl Harbour and that of a scant year and a half later is the difference between two ages in historical time. According to Admiral W.H.P. Blandy, Chief of the U.S. Navy Bureau of Ordance, the latter ship had a defence effectiveness against close-in air attack (the kind that really mattered) some 100 times as great as the former. The guns which comprised the latter's entire defence against such attack, the 40 mm. and the 20 mm. automatic cannon ("machine-guns" in Navy terminology) were not even present on the former ship ; the numbers of those guns were far greater than the numbers of the comparable but inferior guns on the earlier vessel and the means of directing their fire was enormously in advance of the equipment being used in 1941.

Though even the sturdiest of military planes is not capable of sustaining much injury, its swift three-dimensional movement gives it marvellous powers of evasion ; and the task of anti-aircraft fire control has therefore been to predict the position of the target plane at the end of the time it takes for the projectile to arrive in its vicinity. Put in more technical terms, the task is to compute the proper "lead angle" for the guns. Similar problems are of course involved in the control of surface fire between opposing warships but the time permitted for computation and readjustment is much greater, and the splashes of shells give definite spots upon which corrections can be made. In firing against aircraft, the ordinary problems of fire control are greatly augmented as to appear to uninitiated hopeless of solution, which explains the popular tendency toward scorn of the whole anti-aircraft effort, but with modern refinements of anti-aircraft control the problem is far from hopeless. Sights and directors which computed accurate lead angle automatically and quickly were by the middle of 1942 in common use.

It must, of course, be remembered that all the means of anti-aircraft defence will be used together in so far as they are available. If fighter planes are at hand, they will strive to weaken or destroy the enemy's formations long before he comes within the attacking range. Their success will depend mainly on the measure of their strength as compared with that of the enemy attack, though it sometimes happens that the enemy will succeed in eluding one's fighter defence entirely. As the enemy approaches he will first come under the fire of one's 5-inch and 3-inch dual purpose guns and whatever other medium and large calibre guns can be adapted to anti-aircraft defence. The 5-inch DP gun, incidentally, has now become the standard secondary or "broadside" armament of the American battleship and large cruiser. If the attack assumes the character of high level bombing, the 5-inch DPs will perhaps be the only ones that can reach him and these can usually be depended upon at least to impede his aim. But if the enemy resorts to dive bombing or torpedo dropping, the heavy machine-guns, 40 mm, 1.1.-inch and 20 mm, will take up the brunt of the defence. (The number of these guns on our large ships particularly our battleships, cannot now be mentioned, but it is of almost unbelievable magnitude. And their effectiveness is reflected in the results of the battle of Santa Cruz in November 1942, when one of our new battleships shot down 32 Japanese planes in less than that number of minutes of fighting time, meanwhile taking on its armour only one bomb hit which did practically no damage.) Meanwhile the ships will be manoeuvring drastically to dodge the missiles dropped.

The invention which must finally be mentioned and which is basic to all anti-aircraft defence is radar. This marvellous device has robbed the airplane of what once was its chief advantage—the ability to achieve surprise. American naval vessels, equipped with radar, are aided greatly in their anti-aircraft gunnery defence. The distance and bearing of enemy planes can be ascertained while they are still many miles away. Fighter planes can then be despatched to intercept them and all gunnery stations manned and made ready long before they come within view.

With the aid of these devices and weapons, the anti-aircraft defences of warships had by the middle of 1943 reached a high stage of effectiveness. This was especially true of American crafts which were far superior, in this vital respect at least, to their Japanese enemies. Complete immunity even of the largest and most powerfully armed ships was of course not achieved and probably was not achievable. But whether or not complete immunity is attained is relatively unimportant. Any ship can be sunk bv an air attack of sufficiently overwhelming proportions, just as it can be sunk by a torpedo-boat attack of overwhelming proportions. What is important is the number of attacking units necessary to overwhelm. For it may prove physically impossible to marshal that number in or over the battlefield. Besides, it is necessary to consider the relative efficiency of different means of attack. And efficiency must be determined in terms not of unit cost alone but of a whole series of factors which include longevity of individual types, resources available for their construction and operation, rate of wastage in service and especially combat versatility and adaptation to varying geographical and meteorological circumstances.

If the airplane could do everything the ship could do and with greater efficiency, the anti-aircraft effort would still be justified by the fact that large fleets of ships already exist. Ships in hand should be utilized for what they are worth, even if their value has diminished relatively to other and newer forms of war. On the other hand, there would be no justification for building more warships. To be sure, the effectiveness of anti-aircraft fire is itself the gauge by which the value of the sea-borne ship as opposed to the air-borne type is largely determined. For it stands to reason that a fleet of ships which is able to weather any practicable form of air attack without undue attrition will dominate the seas until it is opposed by a superior fleet of ships. But there are other and important reasons why Great Britain and the United States have continued to build warships of generally traditional type as fast as their shipyards can turn them out.

The airplane owes its success as an attack weapon to several characteristics. Its speed enables it to overtake any vessel within its cruising radius. And, prior to the widespread use of radar at any rate, speed enabled it also to gain the advantage of surprise and get in telling blows before the means of resistance available could be organized. Its elevation above the target and thus its ability to utilize the force of gravity enables it to discharge missiles of a size that would require a very large gun and therefore a large ship to hurl. (It should be remembered, however, that the armour-penetrating power and the accuracy of aerial bombs are generally much less than that of gun fire.) The airplane's small size and extreme velocity of movement make it an uncommonly difficult target to hit, which not only helps it in its bombing forays but also serves to make it the best means of torpedo attack against major warships. It can also hope over various kinds of defensive barriers just as the submarine can dive under other types, which means that it can often attack ships in harbours which are adequately defended against other forms of attack. And like the submarine, it is a means of striking blows against forces which by any kind of accounting are vastly superior in strength.

This is a formidable list of advantages, and they have added up to a host of marvellous accomplishments. If these advantages were not balanced at least in part by certain inherent limitations, there would be no question that the day of the surface warship would be over. Every military implement has certain limitations and it does not therefore detract from the value of the airplane to mention those peculiar to it. Such mention merely happens at the present time to be unpopular, with the result that too much is expected of the airplane by itself, and those supporting weapons which are necessary to give it its maximum effectiveness are often passed off in the public mind as relatively useless.

The most obvious limitation of the airplane in naval use is its short endurance which has already been noted in the case of the fighter type but which is inherent in heavier-than-air flying craft generally. The air plane differs fundamentally from the sea-borne vessel or the lighter-than-air type in that a large part of its fuel load is expended not in locomotion but in keeping the craft aloft. And even if that were not true, the fact that the airplane must maintain a high rate of speed for ordinary cruising means that its sea-keeping ability is bound to be limited. For the purposes of escorting a convoy or patrolling areas far removed from one's base, it may be far more important to be able to keep station than to cruise at 200 miles per hour.

The airplane is also far more handicapped by bad weather than the surface warship. Various types of weather conditions will make flight impossible and in certain important maritime regions like the North Sea, such conditions are for from infrequent. This factor alone would suffice to make the surface warship indispensable, at least as an auxiliary, so long as it was at all possible to keep any substantial number afloat in the face of the air threat.

The vulnerability of the airplane has also already been noted, but while it has consequences of more immediate strategic importance, it reflects also on the popular but mistaken assumption that the airplane is generally a cheaper means of doing the same thing which a warship can do. The public eye is concentrated on the single plane which makes the torpedo hit, yet we know that it usually takes large numbers of aircraft to accomplish decisive results and that they often suffer terrible losses in doing so. And the effort and costly organization required to bring an air force to an active area and maintain it in action there usually go quite unnoticed. The vulnerability of aircraft also means that they are a relatively unreliable means of securing results even within their cruising radius. Spectacular successes are matched by costly failures, even in combats which are otherwise exactly comparable. Though the attrition achieved by the successes is always valuable, there are specific instances in which one cannot afford to fail ; and some means which is certain to achieve results must be at hand.

It has been argued by some air enthusiasts that the airplane will completely displace the warship as soon as it is designed with sufficient range to enable it to make itself felt over all portions of the sea while operating from land bases. But the only way the airplane can attain substantially longer range while retaining its ability to carry an appreciable military load, is by increasing its dimensions, and the larger the plane becomes, the more it begins to lose its peculiar virtues. The larger plane is far more expensive per unit and, unlike the surface ship, its invulnerability does not increase proportionately to its size. It is one thing to use large planes to bomb great cities at night and quite another to use them over the sea in daylight against moving targets which may include powerfully armed warships. It has been proved again and again in all the active maritime theatres of this war that the kind of plane which achieves decisive results on the high seas is not the big bomber which bombs from level flight at high altitude, but the divebomber and the torpedo plane, and these must for tactical reasons be small planes. Only when ship targets are stationary in harbours or abysmally lacking in anti-aircraft armament or other defences—which the more modern warships are not – can the large bombers be counted upon to secure results.

Besides, the more one emphasizes range in the design of a plane, the more one must sacrifice characteristics which are tactically desirable, such as speed, manoeuvrability, rate of climb and armament load. The larger the plane, the larger the field required for its take-off and there are many important areas of the globe – the Solomon Islands, for instance—where landing fields are so scarce that any flat, open space becomes the object of bitter campaigns. The large plane is even more hampered by adverse weather than the small one since there are fewer fields available for emergency landings. Finally, how much range would it take to enable a land-based plane to attend a convoy moving across the ocean—assuming that a plane which could keep station with a convoy was tactically adequate to beating off various kinds of attackers?

The fighting in the Solomon Islands in the autumn and winter of 1942-43 put the limitations of the plane in sharp relief. The scarcity of aircraft carriers because of losses and the even greater scarcity of airdromes greatly limited the number of aircraft which could be put over the fighting lines or landing beaches. We had only Henderson Field on Guadalcanal. Australia is much too far to permit large bombers sent from there to keep the air over Guadalcanal and, of course, divebombers or torpedo planes could not fly the round-trip distance at all. The result was that even in this outstanding example of amphibious operations, where aircraft are generally at their maximum effectiveness, the airplane by no means stole the show from the surface ship.

Considering naval operations as they should be considered, from the viewpoint of the long haul rather than merely of the coastal operation, it is clear that the land-based airplane cannot dominate the seas unless the devastation it accomplishes in terminal or coastal areas, is of such proportions that events on the broad seas become relatively unimportant. Such a condition has by no means yet come into being. The destruction of shipping by aircraft in coastal areas has taken place on a large scale, but at least as concerns United Nations shipping it has fallen far short of being decisive. There have been exceptions in the case of particular campaigns and along particularly exposed routes, but in general the proposition is true.

The same applies to warships, especially major warships including the much-abused battleships. Thus far the Prince of Wales and Repulse and possibly one Japanese battleship have been the only capital ships which have been struck down entirely from the air while at sea, and this in more than three years of war. The quantity and quality of anti-aircraft defence on battleships has improved enormously in the period which has elapsed since, and it is bound to improve further. A great deal might be added on this question, both pro and con, but all these arguments would pale into insignificance beside the fundamental fact that a Luftwaffe immensely superior to the Royal Air Force for two long years and based on nearby Norway and France did not wrest control of the Atlantic from Britain. What would have happened, however, if the Germans had had a navy superior to the British Navy in fighting power ?

Any unbiased observer must concede that the airplane or the warship can stand on its abilities to do things which the other can do either less well or not at all and it is obvious that the margin of utility of each is very great. Campaigns in narrow waters have in some instances been determined by air supremacy. Powerful anti-aircraft defence is not always available to groups of small warships or merchant vessels. In the anti-submarine campaign in the Atlantic, the airplane in United Nations hands has proved of crucial value. But it is particularly in the latter type of work that the interdependence of air and surface work has been demonstrated. Due to its ability to cover large areas in brief periods of time, the airplane has made it necessary for German U-boats to keep constantly on the alert in combat areas and for the most part submerged during daylight hours. The latter fact especially has been an enormous hindrance to U-boats in their operations. But due to the limitations of aircraft in sea-keeping endurance and in depthcharge load, and due especially to their inability to detect submarines below periscope depth, far the greater number of kills at sea have been accomplished by surface craft. The airplane has, of course, often been responsible for calling to the scene the surface vessels which finished the job. It is the team which accomplishes the objective and it is to the team that the credit must be given.

The use of the airplane in anti-submarine work underlines its value as a reconnaissance agent. Almost every aerial bomb which strikes home makes the first-page news but the accomplishments of the aerial observer are generally passed over in silence. Yet it might be doubted that the reconnaissance value of aircraft adds up to less than their attack value. The two cannot as a rule be separated but great decisions have been made and large operations put in progress on the basis of what was seen from the air.

Even when atmospheric conditions are such that visibility is not enhanced by taking a position aloft—which is often the case—the speed of the airplane enables it to reconnoiter large areas in a short time. On the trans-Atlantic ferry, it has been invaluable not only spotting U-boats on the surface or at periscope depth but also for bringing together portions of convoys which have been scattered by attack and which are enjoined to radio silence. It has helped convoys also to contact warship escorts sent out to meet them. And its ability to dash in where warships fear to tread has enabled fleets to keep check on the enemy's dispositions and oarticularly on the whereabouts of his major warships. The Bismarck was not long out of Bergen when her departure was discovered.

As an instrument of reconnaissance, however, the airplane seems on the whole to favour the command of the superior fleet. The British have been able, largely because of the reconnaissance airplane, to command the North Atlantic under conditions (*i.e.*, German occupation of the French and Norwegian coasts) which would have made such command impossible in World War I. There are exceptions to this general rule, to be sure, particularly since the reconnaissance airplane may be the advance agent not for a fleet but for an air force which is determined to challenge the domination of a fleet. Nevertheless, if the utility of the airplane were confined to reconnaissance, the traditional patterns of strategy would be if anything more solidified and strengthened than formerly.

The development of naval aviation has called into being the aircraft carrier, the only really new type of major combatant vessel introduced in the twentieth century. Strategically considered, it is a warship like other warships save that its primary weapons are airplanes instead of gunds. It is a vessel in which the mobility peculiar to surface fleets and that peculiar to aircraft are combined. The airplane, while extremely mobile within cruising radius of its base, is tied to that base by a relatively short tether and the amount of military work it can do in a single sortie, is markedly limited. The large warship, on the other hand, though much slower moving than the aircraft, enjoys a much greater cruising radius and is immeasurably more self-contained while at sea.

Despite the very considerable losses in this type of warship suffered by the three major naval belligerents in World War II, no other type could show a more brilliant record of accomplishment, especially when measured in terms of tangible damage inflicted upon the enemy per ship engaged. The toll taken by submarines has been much greater in the mass but there have been far larger numbers of submarines at sea than aircraft carriers.

After its amazing achievements in the first year of the Pacific campaign, particularly in the battles of the Coral Sea and Midway Islands, the aircraft carrier became in the popular view and in a good portion of naval opinion as well, the "backbone of the fleet." It was considered to have clearly demonstrated its superiority in tactical efficiency to the previously acknowledged queen, the battleship.

That the aircraft carrier has proved itself pre-eminent in ability to inflict damage is beyond dispute. That it is bound to remain of enormous tactical importance in war at sea is also beyond question. Aircraft are not likely to increase so much in sea keeping endurance as to make the carrier unnecessary; nor, on the other hand, are they likely to lose so much in ability to destroy as to rob it of its utility.

But that the aircraft carrier has displaced the battleship as the arbiter of the great and decisive battles has, by no means, been proved at this writing. The questions involved are strategic as well as tactical. For example, where one's total forces are insufficient to gain real command, a carrier or a few sub-marines acting as raiders may be much more valuable than a battleship. And the fact that the strategic value of a line of battleships is out of all proportion to the number of occasions in which it engages in battle is also likely to obscure the true scale of values between the types. Thus far the carrier has shown brightest in what were essentially raiding operations, embodying so far as the United States was concerned a fundamentally defensive strategic policy. Whether it would enjoy the same prominence in a show-down fight for command of the sea is, however, doubtful. To win such an offensive campaign, carriers would have to overwhelm the main strength of the enemy battle fleet.

Tactically, the number of considerations relevant to the problem is legion but a few may be isolated as of prime importance. First among these is the question of the efficiency of anti-aircraft fire. It is too often forgotten that the carrier suffers not only from its own relative vulnerability which is inherent in its function, but also from the vulnerability of its offensive agents. Its offensive power can be frustrated not only by attack planes and surface gunfire, as is true of other ships, but also by anti-aircraft fire and fighter planes. Incidentally, it is usually too readily assumed that the carrier will never come under the gunfire of enemy surface forces. The Glarious was quickly destroyed by the fire of the Gneisenau and Scharnkorst, and during one phase of the Battle of the Coral Sea our carrier force discovered a Japanese force only 30 miles away. There is reason to believe that the avoidance of a gun action at that time was the deliberate choice of the American admiral rather than something enjoined by circumstances.

Although the hitting power of the carrier extends as far as the range of the bombing and torpedo planes which take off from it, it must be remembered that its volume of fire at extended ranges is very low when compared with the battleship. The latter can hurl in one hour a weight of heavy projectiles which would require perhaps 800 carrier-type planes to carry and those projectiles would have an accuracy and armour-penetrating force unknown to bombing. Naturally, if the carrier's aircraft attack with torpedoes, its effectiveness must be weighed in terms other than those implying comparison with gunfire ; but, on the other hand, it is too often forgotten that the recently demonstrated effectiveness of torpedoes against large warships may be a transitory phenomenon. Torpedo planes have already proved to be the type most easily shot down, and the slow speed of the missile is a major handicap. Speedy vessels—and all modern battleships are speedy—are extremely difficult targets to hit with torpedoes even at close range. Finally, certain structural changes, some of which have already been accomplished, promise to reduce greatly the destructive power of those torpedoes which do strike.

The offensive power of the carrier is far more inhibited than that of gunships by darkness or adverse weather. On the day the Bismarck was finally destroyed, the aircraft of the Ark Royal which had attacked her successfully the previous day were unable to take off because of heavy seas. And the vulnerability of the carrier to any form of attack is something which defies ultimate solution. Heavy armour cannot be placed above the hangar deck, which means that all the fighting facilities of the craft are exposed. The large quantities of gasoline stored in the ship and in the tanks of its aircraft constitute a great fire hazard. And the fact that the carrier must turn into the wind and maintain a steady course while launching or receiving its planes, means that it is an easy target during those periods.

In the end, it is possible that the tactical career of the aircraft carrier will approximate that of the tank in land warfare. The tank enjoyed supreme ascendancy during the campaigns of 1939-41, for the simple reason that defensive tactics against it were not sufficiently advanced. In those days the tank was really the "spearhead of attack," but events in Africa in 1942-43 indicated that the situation had changed radically to the tank's disadvantage. It is still, and will probably remain, a vitally important element in modern land forces but the day when it had things all its own way, is gone forever. The same may be true of carriers by the time those projected at this writing are completed.

Naturally, if Japanese anti-aircraft fire could be counted upon to remain as bad as it was in the Battle of the Bismarck Sea of March 1943, it might be wise to plan upon overwhelming their battle fleet with a fleet of carriers. But one cannot, and the United States Navy in fact does not, count upon such a contingency. A great modern fleet of American battleships is at this writing coming into being and will take its place beside the fleet of aircraft carriers that is also rapidly being completed. The combination of the two is bound to be a far more effective and efficient method of winning battles than reliance upon either one alone.

It must finally be borne in mind that so long as the influence of the airplane is felt over the seas, air power is not something distinct from sea power but an integral part of it. Thus, advances in the tactical efficiency of aircraft cannot diminish the dominant influence upon modern global war of sea power, which refers merely to the ability to control seaborne transportation over the seas. And the hitting force exerted by air-craft operating from advanced bases gives new importance to the sea power which makes it possible to seize, hold and supply those bases.

Of course, the strategic framework in which sea power operates, has changed enormously as a result of the airplane. Not all of this change redounds to the disadvantage of sea power by any means. The strategic bombing of Germany, for example, is closely integrated with the Anglo-American blockade. The bombing takes up where the blockade leaves off and the effectiveness of the combination is vastly greater than either one would be by itself. On the other hand, it is true that the danger of aerial invasion or at least raiding of an island like Great Britain does mean that the British Fleet can no longer guarantee almost by itself the security of the British Isles, though the continuing importance of its protection is generally underrated. The fact that the British Isles were not invaded in 1940 could hardly be due exclusively to a British air force which was far inferior in power to the German Luftwaffe, nor could it be due to a British army which was disorganized and virtually disarmed.

The question of whether the airplane will eventually replace the surface merchant vessel as the carrier of the bulk of ocean commerce needs also to be answered, though there has been a good deal of rank nonsense written on the subject. If such a change should occur, sea power as we have known it in the past will no longer have any reason for being. The most that can be said today, however, is that such a change, if it is at all possible, is still far in the future.

CHAPTER NINE

WAR IN THE DETERRENT AGE

A major preoccupation of statesman and military leaders during the past 20 years has been to try to determine, by analysis and rationalization, what would be the nature of future wars and what types of armed forces would be required to fight them. There have been wide variances in assessment not only between ally and ally but also between the armed forces themselves—differences that have led to considerable friction in the defence services.

During the first few years of the nuclear age, there was widespread belief in Western countries that conventional types of wars had become outdated— a belief that is held in many quarters even today. At the same time, those who admit the likelihood of conventional wars tend to swing to the other extreme and assume that the old characteristics of conventional tactics would persist even under a nuclear umbrella (though intensified by the threat of nuclear weaponry).

Almost 80 years ago, a military philosopher, a pacifist Polish Jew called I.S. Bloch, wrote a six-volume treatise on war in which he tried to persuade warlike nations that the ever-increasing power of modern weaponry had eliminated war as an instrument of policy :

> What is the use of talking about the past when you are dealing with an altogether new set of circumstances ? The

> first thing that war would do would be to deprive the powers that made it of all opportunity of benefiting by the products of the nations against whom they were fighting... Humanity has progressed beyond the stage in which war can any longer be regarded as a possible Court of Appeal.

Bloch was moved to write his thesis because he was appalled by the destructive power of the new weapons of those days—the magazine rifle, the machine-gun and quick-firing artillery. Today, the warlike nations of the world face not only battle-field destruction but wholesale extermination of civilized existence. Virtually nothing of human creation could survive in the target areas of a multi-megaton bombardment. There would be nothing left to gain or acquire ; the means would have swallowed the end. Can anyone assume with any degree of conviction that a sane political aim could be achieved by wielding a force of this nature ?

And yet a basic assumption in today's super-power strategy is that it is possible for a future war to start with an all-out surprise nuclear attack and therefore each must be in a position to wipe out the other before being wiped out itself.

Reasoning and analysis obviously have not been able to eliminate the possibility of the absure war. Perhaps the time will come when a more stable nuclear balance, based on multi-lateral rather than bilateral deterrents and enforced through the agency of some form of international computer system, will succeed in doing what human logic has so far failed to do—totally rule out the possibility of mutual annihilation ; but for the present, the possibility remains. The only hopeful element in this climate of ultimate war possibilities is that as the horror weapons become bigger and stockpiles increase on each side, the likelihood of their being unleashed becomes smaller and smaller.

But in this hope also there is danger ; over-reliance on the deterrent power of nuclear weapons builds a psychological resistance towards planning for other forms of war. This was the attitude of the United States during the earlier fifties ; and European NATO largely clings to it today. Dependence on the big bombs has offered a convenient excuse for neglecting the lesser weapons of war.

Military policy in the nuclear age must condition itself to a new phenomenon of strategy. In the past, nations waged war on a predictable, logical basis – they used their maximum weapons potential to achieve their aim. One of the basic principles of conventional war is that of concentration of forces—in other words, use of maximum manpower and firepower. But today the basis has changed : the strategy of nuclear deterrence induces an inhibition that compels even the most powerful nation to confine its military execution to a level of warfare below that of its maximum potential. Not only that ; the paradox stretches further. It is normally the aggressor who, in order to minimize the retaliatory action of the defender, will seek the lower levels of war ; and it is the defender who will more easily exercise an option on the level at which to retaliate.

One of the main factors that emerge from the arguments and hypotheses of nuclear dialectics, particularly when considering the possible levels of future war, is uncertainty—uncertainty of the enemy's capability ; uncertainty of his motivation, his will to enforce the deterrent, and uncertainty of his estimate of one's own resources and one's own motivation. Any strategy that is devised for the future must therefore pay full regard to this factor of uncertainty and endeavour to encompass the whole range of possibilities that it implies. Adherence to an attitude as inflexible as those of the past runs counter to such a requirement.

It is true that reliance on the certainty of absolute deterrence appears increasingly feasible as the horror weapons become more and more destructive. But even supposing that absolute deterrence has been acknowledged by both sides, it is the ultimate exchange that will have been deterred – not other forms of war. In fact, from the de-escalation perspective, it is the very stability of mutual deterrence at the top that encourages freedom of action at lower levels ; and if that be so, the aim of opposing power blocs in future will be to seek new areas in which to take warlike actions—offensive and defensive—that could at the same time achieve an aim and yet avoid escalation to unacceptable levels. Thus, an aggressor's object would be to launch an offensive at the lowest level of warfare at which he can gain and advantage ; while the defender's aim would be to whittle down the aggressor's freedom of action by using the threat of escalation as a deterrence.

In order to examine the complete spectrum of choices that has been created under the stability umbrella of the bilateral deterrents, we must proceed beyond the range of what we had previously termed "limited wars". It is necessary to enlarge that perspective and include, for the present purpose, the whole ascending scale of warlike actions that start in peace-time and stretch upwards to strategic nuclear warfare ; and for the purpose of our analysis, this increased perspective will be considered in three broad categories—cold war, tactical war and strategic war.

One of the consequences of adjustment from the traditional concept of war strategy to that of the strategy of deterrence has been that peace has now become far more stable. Where previously international tensions would inevitably have resulted in open hostilities, today even such extremely serious situations as the confrontment over Berlin or the Cuban crisis are settled by compromise. To that extent, therefore, the nuclear age has brought with it stability even at the lower levels of war. At the same time, however, the old notion of peace has lost its absolute character ; in the deterrent age peace includes almost continuous situations of covert but positive actions that might range from virulent propaganda to subversive guerrilla offensives in the guise of national uprisings. It is this range of hostile actions, camouflaged as peace, which we term "cold war".

The main characteristic that distinguishes cold war from the other two categories is that cold war cannot be deterred ; in fact, it is the very threat of deterrence that forces certain forms of violence to convert from overt to covert form ; they then become disguised as cold war—that is, warlike actions during peace.

Continuing the analysis of cold war characteristics, it will be seen that the more remote the deterrent, the more latitude cold war will seek. Thus, if the only deterrent to cold war actions is a nuclear threat (as was the case in Europe after the West's conventional forces were demobilized following World War II) its range increases considerably and can include such direct forms as the Berlin blockade or, in extreme cases, even minor take-over bids. On the other hand, if cold war action is deterred by a more immediate (even if less powerful) deterrent such as conventional retaliation, its range is considerably reduced. This phenomenon is a corollary of the strategy of deterrence and has found acceptance in Russia and the United States, but only with reservations in Europe.

Experience during certain crises in the past has proved that in the age of deterrents not only can cold war moves extend over a wide range of possible actions but, in certain circumstances, they can influence decisions at even the tactical level. A good example of this was the pressure brought to bear by Russia on the British and French governments during their Suez venture. Although Khrushchev had hinted about possible nuclear action, it did not amount to using the deterrence : it was mainly through cold war pressures that he forced the Anglo-French offensive to a halt.

In the next category—that is, tactical war—conventional and tactical nuclear wars have been grouped together not only because of their common characteristics of tactical combat potential but also because, unlike cold war, tactical war can be deterred and, unlike the strategic forces, tactical forces do not in themselves constitute an "absolute" deterrent.

It will be obvious that this is not an operational grouping that we have made ; rather, it is categorization arising from the notion of deterrence. For example, from the operational point of view, cold war actions can, in fact, take the form of minor conventional war such as subversive guerilla offensives, border violations or creeping territorial encroachment. Before the age of deterrents these same operations, even at a low level of application, would have been construed as acts of war ; but today they are an almost continuous, covert process and are accepted as cold war actions. It is the dialogue of escalation and deterrence that makes this possible.

Let us examine next the conditions under which tactical-level wars—that is, conventional war or tactical nuclear war—can take place. Here, also, we see a basic difference in characteristic between cold war and tactical-level war. Under the notion of deterrence, cold war is a continuous process, even if its range of warlike actions can, in certain circumstances, be reduced. On the other hand, the possibility of wars at the tactical level is a variable factor dependent on the degree of nuclear stability established by the strategic deterrents. Thus, as we saw in a previous chapter, in a hypothetical situation of absolute instability (in other words, when the opposing first-strike threats become entirely credible) the likelihood of conventional or tactical nuclear wars approaches zero ; but the very disappearance of this likelihood increases the range of actions at the cold war level.

Lastly, the difference in characteristics between tactical-level war and strategic war is a fundamental one of function. War at the tactical level has an actual operational function—to gain ascendancy over the enemy's forces in combat. Accordingly, tactical forces are those that are primarily designed for actual combat and not for "political" purposes. The function of strategic strike forces, on the other hand, is primarily one of deterrence—that is, they are designed to prevent war, not fight it. Strategic war is, therefore, a conception of war in which the prime requirement for its forces should be that they must never actually be used.

It has not been the purpose here merely to indulge in a dialectic of action and deterrence but to establish a logical basis upon which strategic planning and military policy can be effectively undertaken. It is only too obvious in the world today that because military policy is often formulated from obsolete concepts or emotional attitudes, there exist serious divergencies and divisive trends even among the closest allies. It is only if future policy can be based on logically derived rules and formulae of nuclear strategy that there can be some hope of accord and agreement in military plans and preparation to meet the threat of aggression from the expanding nations.

Let us now see how the arguments and conclusions set

forth above can be translated into concrete ideas on which military planning could be based.

To begin with, we can suggest a set of general principles that might be applicable under the notion of deterrence in a bilateral confrontment :

Strategic war is an instrument of deterrence, not a predictable function ;
the deterrent influence of strategic forces extends only to the tactical level and not to cold war actions, which are a continuous process and cannot be deterred ;
tactical-level war is a predictable function, the range of forms it might take varying in direct proportion to the degree of stability generated by the strategic forces ; and
the existence of an effective tactical-level capability, though it cannot deter cold war, reduces its range of warlike actions.

If these principles are accepted, it becomes possible to test the validity of the various types of military policy that have been suggested or adopted by the democratic nations in order to counter the threat of aggression from the eastern bloc.

Firstly, there is the "massive retaliation" type of policy—that is, a type that disregards the necessity of maintaining large tactical forces and plans instead to counter a major tactical-level threat by the application of the strategic deterrent. We have discussed the "political" and "military" implications and the validity of such a policy in a previous chapter, but here its cold war liability must also be considered. Even if the "massive retaliation" threat were credible—that is, the strategic deterrent possessed a known superiority over the aggressor's—this policy possesses the inherent disadvantage that the very de-emphasis of tactical forces gives the aggressor the choice of a wide range of cold war actions ; the aggressor might well find it possible to achieve his aim (or part-aim) without having to "aggress" at all, because a defensive status quo power would not unleash a strategic first-strike merely to counter cold war actions, even if they assumed serious proportions.

This disadvantage became apparent during the early years of NATO, when its tactical capability was much smaller than that of Russia. The result was that even under a credible U.S. "massive retaliation" policy, a wide latitude of cold war options could be exercised by the Russians—an advantage that was so effectively exploited during the Berlin crisis.

Then there is the type of military policy that has empirically developed in NATO or at least in European NATO - that is, the maintenance of just sufficient tactical forces to deter or halt an initial aggression ; but to defeat it reliance is placed on the U.S. strategic deterrent. Besides, even within the broad terms of this policy, European members of NATO argue that for such a tactical force, a nuclear element is more necessary than the conventional element because the former possesses a deterrent potential while the latter does not.

If we examine this policy in the light of the general principles mentioned above, two major disadvantages at once become apparent. Firstly, the absence of a strong conventional element in the tactical forces would still provide an aggressor with a large range of cold war actions (though not as large as in the first case). But the main disadvantage is that it presupposes a high degree of credibility of the U.S. deterrent—a credibility that no longer exists under the stability equation that has been established between the U.S. and Soviet strategic forces. Reliance on this policy under the existing nuclear situation would, therefore, mean that the response mechanism of NATO to a determined cold war action by the Warsaw powers would be limited ; in fact, its only course of action would be to escalate the conflict to tactical nuclear level. The likelihood of this escalation is further increased by the fact that the areas that would be affected by tactical nuclear war are "marginal" areas and not the home territories of the two superpowers.

In these circumstances, there are two alternative requirements that could restore the imbalance and, thus, induce stability at lower levels. The first is the need to increase the conventional element of NATO's tactical forces so that the range of hostile cold war actions can be reduced ; and the second is what the French have anyway decided to do—that is, inject an independent "third party" strategic deterrent into the bilateral system. This "independent" deterrent would have the effect of creating just that degree of instability in the superpowers equation that is required to prevent low-level conflicts from automatically escalating to large-scale tactical nuclear war; and it is in this context that General De Gaulle's nuclear policy gains validity (though it would have been even more convincing had he at the same time taken steps to increase the conventional potential of NATO by supporting it with French divisions rather than undermining it by pulling them out).

Whatever the case, the element of uncertainty cannot altogether be eliminated from this NATO type of policy. In fact the only policy that can restore full flexibility in the response mechanism and largely eliminate the factor of uncertainty is the policy that the United States advocates but cannot wholly pursue in Europe because of NATO resistance—that is, to maintain a complex of armed forces designed to defeat all forms of aggression at their own level.

It is not impossible for the combined resources of the Western powers to match the conventional capability of the Warsaw Pact; but what European NATO argues is that such a conventional capability would be largely meaningless unless it were given the power to use tactical nuclear weapons without having to depend upon U.S. decisions. This has created the west-west crisis today. France plans to break it by influencing it with a "third party" independent deterrent, even if it be a "minimum deterrent," and it is not inconceivable that at some future date, Britain can be persuaded to disentangle her nuclear capability from its present dependence on America and throw in her lot with France in her "third party" policy.

However, in spite of the lead given by France, the creation of a "European deterrent" is as yet a remote possibility. The eventual solution of the purely nuclear aspect of the problem will inevitably be influenced by a number of other factors, not least among them being the effect that a future Chinese strategic capability will have on the U.S.—Russian bilateral stability. But, irrespective of the eventual nuclear development, what needs to be emphasized now is the importance of maintaining an adequate conventional capability to ensure stability over the whole range of warlike actions.

From our analysis of nuclear possibilities, it has become clear that the likely form that a future war would take cannot be forecast with any degree of exactitude. Unlike military strategy in the past, nuclear strategy cannot be regarded as a rigid, morphic structure on the basis of which methods of execution can be predicted. It is a shifting, adaptable concept which can produce a multiplicity of possible courses, to meet which the only effective policy would be one that objectively envisages the whole gamut of military actions.

The old form of military strategy implied the adoption of a course, based on the principles of war, that would harness the maximum resources of a nation to gain a swift and decisive victory. Today, strategy is a variable concept based on the interaction of escalation and deterrence; and the forms in which a war is likely to be fought will vary within the range of options that the escalation-limits permit.

Let us consider the problem faced by status quo powers threatened by aggression under the umbrella of deterrence. The ascending scale of threatened aggression starts at the cold war scale conventional forms. Defensive policy to meet this aggression will initially consist of controlled escalation in three different forms: firstly, an increase in the intensity of the conflict—in other words, a quantitative escalation within the same form of action, such as was done in the first phase of America's war in Vietnam, secondly, a widening of the area of conflict, such as retaliatory raids (bombing of North Vietnam, as in the present phase); and, thirdly, political escalation—that is, taking retaliatory action (on the same level) in an entirely different area where the military confrontment is more advantageous. Thus, if the Americans were to launch a conventional-type attack on Matsu and Quemoy to relieve pressure on South Vietnam this would constitute "political escalation".

So far, escalation strategy has remained within the limits of conventional responses. The options within this level are themselves wide but they presuppose a conventional capability strong enough to match the aggressor's. If this condition is fulfilled, as in Vietnam today, a kind of "agreed battle" situation results which obviates the necessity of "brinkmanship", that is, escalation to the nuclear level. But "agreed battle" strategy would not be feasible in a parallel confrontment in Europe where the conventional superiority of the Warsaw powers would inevitably lead to situations in which they could force a decision at that level; and the only alternative left to the defenders would be to escalate to the tactical nuclear level.

The likelihood of tactical nuclear combat under an effective deterrent has already been discussed. It only needs to be mentioned in the present context that tactical-level war is, unlike strategic war, a form that is predictable and for which preparation has been made (or should have been made). It is too easily assumed today that nuclear war can never take place, notwithstanding the fact that such an assumption cancels the very credibility of the nuclear deterrent. To combine dialectics with realism, a much more logical assumption is that nuclear war is, in fact, possible but that it would probably start at a very low level of intensity—that is, in combination with conventional war—and that (except in circumstances nearing absolute instability) a compromise would be reached well before the level of full-scale tactical nuclear war. But in order to possess the response mechanism of such a "sub-limited" nuclear war, a strong conventional capability is necessary—a conclusion from which European NATO has persistently shied away.

Inability or unwillingness to plan for war at lower levels created a weakness in defensive policy that could present an aggressor with the very opportunity he seeks, that is, freedom of cold war or conventional actions. The Warsaw Pact powers maintain tactical forces that at their peak could field up to 150 divisions in Europe, capable of both conventional and tactical nuclear warfare. To meet this potential threat, it had been agreed at the Lisbon Conference that an eventual total of some 96 divisions would be required for the defence of Europe; and of this number some 35 to 40 divisions would have to be permanently maintained "on the line". However, western Europe has hesitated to face these targets. This was understandable so long as American nuclear strategy was based on Mr. Dulles' all-or-nothing policy. But, in the light of the changes in outlook that have since taken place, inability to meet an enemy's challenge over the whole range of actions at the tactical level creates a strategic weakness that can be compensated only by escalation to strategic war, that is, by recourse to the absurd.

Nor is the European requirement the only demand that could be placed on the tactical forces of NATO. Elements of them in a conventional role (or even in a controlled nuclear role, now that Asia is involved in a nuclear confrontation) might well be necessary for the exercise of Asian military balance. In fact if Western nations intend to sponsor the non-proliferation of nuclear weapons in Asia, such a demand would become irrefutable.

As things stand today, only the United States is in a position to commit forces for the maintenance of military balance in Asia; but it is not inconceivable, in certain possible situations, that that balance could be more effectively restored by a Western power of the non-superpower category, say, Britain or possibly France. Inability to make such a contribution might well create a strategic impasse that the aggressor would be quick to exploit.

Let us now consider one more possible development. Despite Western pressures, one of the stable status quo powers in Asia might still decide to develop its own nuclear capacity—with the object of neutralizing China's monopoly. Would this alter the requirement for Western conventional support ?

It is not unreasonable to assume that once a nuclear "argument" starts in Asia, a state of mutual deterrence within the purely Asian setting would eventually be established. But, just as is the case in the present East-West balance, it would be the nuclear exchange that would have been deterred—not conventional aggression. And in that sphere no Asian nation, not even a group of nations, is likely to achieve parity with China whose freedom of action for a venture at lower levels of warfare would be as great as it is today. Thus, the military balance (even under a nuclear stability umbrella) would again be entirely dependent on western conventional support.

Looked at from any angle, therefore, the necessity for Western powers to maintain effective tactical forces, that is, forces that can be used for both conventional and tactical nuclear war, is inescapable. More than a necessity, it is a responsibility—a responsibility towards maintaining freedom both in Europe and in Asia. After China's entry in the nuclear scene, Asian strategic problems can no longer be regarded as a separate concept related to traditional rather than nuclear notions.

In point of fact, the Asian requirement reaches down even further than the conventional level. Unlike the European setting, in which both blocs have graduated beyond the guerilla stage, the Chinese Communist government has clearly indicated that large-scale conventional war is, by no means, its main strategy for conducting its expansionist policy. On the contrary, war at an intensity lower than conventional—that is, the guerrilla offensive as a tactical-level concept—might well prove more effective, the present checkmate in North Vietnam notwithstanding. Therefore, until such time as the free world in Asia finds an effective answer to the "unconventional" threat, even the Western-supported conventional balance cannot be regarded as being wholly adequate to prevent China's creeping expansionism.

Unfortunately, there has as yet been no indication of the formation of s. ccessful counter-guerrilla strategy ; in many cases, even the awareness of the need has been lacking. In this sphere, an effective response to the problem must primarily be an Asian responsibility because basically it is more a political than a military problem ; and the continuous conflict between political and military requirements needs to be reflected rather than masked in the material support that the West offers. But, to begin with, there must be an awareness of the task which is neither simple to plan nor cheap or quick to execute.

To quote once more from Bloch, his forecast of future warfare was as follows :

> Then, instead of war fought out to the bitter end in a series of decisive battles, we shall have as a substitute a long period of continually increasing strain upon the resources of the combatants. The war, instead of being a hand-to-hand contest, in which the combatants measure their physical and moral superiority, will become a kind of stalemate,

> in which, neither army being willing to get at the other, threatening the other, but never being able to deliver a final and decisive attack—That is the future of war—not fighting, but famine ; not the slaying of men but the bankruptcy of nations and the break-up of the whole social organisation...

The prediction is almost uncanny: Mao Tse-tung's strategic teaching of guerrilla attrition is but an extension of the "stalemate" of bankruptcy and social disintegration that Bloch foresaw. The Chinese have devised a strategy that uses that very stalemate as a means or waging war ; and if victory is to be wrested from this morass of political warfare the nations that face it, must be aware of the threat and plan and prepare from now for the counter measure.

It has been the purpose in this book to suggest that the establishment of a balance of deterrents in nuclear strategy does not necessarily create a historical condition in which other forms of war become outlawed. On the contrary, we have now entered a new era in history, in which strategic planning entails being prepared at all times to wage wars at all levels, ranging from the "absurd" war of a swift all-out nuclear exchange (that must be planned but regarded as not possible to be fought) to Mao Tse-tung's creeping guerrilla aggression that might involve years of actual but "unconventional" combat.

Unfortunately, the very immensity of the requirement creates a reluctance for its acceptance. It becomes easier to believe that the absolute deterrent is absolute strategy ; so that the choice in future could lie only between mutual destruction and peace and that therefore the threat of the one is the only guarantee of the other.

Perhaps a convincing argument could be offered to support such an outlook ; but there comes a period when dependence on logic must be made conditional—and it just be tested against actuality. In neither Europe nor Asia is there any sign that the acquisition of nuclear power by would-be aggressors has led to a significant de-emphasis on conventional arms. As the confrontment exists on the ground today, the "expanding" nations possess a greater range of flexible alternatives than the status quo powers. From the line of the Iron Curtain in Europe to the frontiers of Communism in South-east Asia, local strategic superiority has nowhere remained in the hands of the democracies. In Asia, this disparity is inherent in the situation ; in Europe, it has been a deliberate choice—in the hope that it is also a short cut to peace and prosperity.

BIBLIOGRAPHY

Presscott. J.R.V., the Geography of State Policies, Hutchinson University Lib., London, 1968.

Cyril. Falls, Geography and war strategy, Geographical Jour. vol. CXII no. 1-3, Jan. 1949.

Raup. H.F., The Impact of air power on geographic Education, The Jour. of Geog. vol. LVI, no. 3, 1957.

Brodie, Bernard, Sea power in the machine Age, 1969.

Thompson. E.R. The Nature of Military Geog : A Preliminary Survey, Syracuse Univ., 1962.

Rampal S.N. Airwar, Trimurti Pub. N.D. 1974.

Peltier. Louis C. and Pearcy. G. Etzel, Military geography, D. Van. Nostrand Co., N.Y., 1966.

Price H. Paul and Woodward Herbert P., Geological Notes, 1942. U.S.A.

Boulding Kenneth E., Peace and the War Industry, Aldine Pub. Co., 1970, U.S.A.

Raloinowitch Eugene and Adams Ruth, Deleate the Antile allistic Missile, Bul. of the Atomic Scientists. 1967. U.S.A.

OSgood. Charles, An Atlernative to War or Surrender, Uni. of Illinois Press, 1963.

Wright. Quincy and Evan William M, Preventing World III, Some proposals, Simson and Schuster, N.Y., 1962.

Woodrow Jacolbs, Wartime Development in Applied Climatology, Ame. Meteo. Soc. Boston, 1947. p. 52.

Jeffries Wn. W., Geography and National Power, U.S Naval. Inst., 1958.

Robert. Strausz Hupe, Geopolitics, the Struggle for Space and Power, N.Y., 1942.

Johnson. Douglas, Topography and Strategy in the War, Bul. of the Amer. Geog. Soc. XLVII (1915)

Ward, Robert. Dec., Meteorology and War, Annals. VIII, 1918.

Belloc. Hilaire, The Geography of the War, Geographical Journal. XLV, 1915.

Devernon. Simson Francois Gay, A Treatise on the Science of War and Fortification, N.Y. 1817, 2. vol.

Schoolmaster, The Military Geography, Chathan, 1889, pp. 122.

Franklin. Capt. T. Bed ford, Tactics and the Land scape, London 1944, pp. 56.

Jackson. Col. J.R., On Military Geography—its Nature, Object and Importance, London. 1850.

May. Col. E.S., Geography in Relation to War, London 1907, pp. 61.

Verner. Capt Willoughlby, Some Notes on Military Topography, London and Calcutta, 1891.

Brooks. A.H., The Influence of Geography on the Conduct of the War, Geographic Review X, July, 1920, pp. 43-55

Johnson, Doughlas, Geographic Aspect of the War, Bal. of the Amer. Geog. Soc. XIVII (1915)

——, Meteorology and War, Annals. VIII, 1918.

Belloc. Hilaire, The Geography of the War, Geog. Journal XLV, 1915

Mackie. Lt. G.B., Geography in Relation to War, Scottish Geog. Mags. No. 11, 12, 1917.

Whitllesey. Derwent, the Role of Geography in Twentieth Century War, N.Y. 194.

Foott. Brig. Gen. C.H., the Influence of Geography on War, Queensland Geog. Jour. XLII—XLIV, 1926-29.

Donoghue. Lt. Col. John. H., The Geography of Total War, Military Engineer, XXXV, July 1943, pp. 334-335.

La Rocque. Alex. J., The Role of Geography in Military Planning, Canadian Geographer III., 1953.

Goutard. Col, Geography and Modern Strategy, Military Review XXIX, June, 1949.

Raynal. Prof., Geographical Studies in Warfare, Military Review XXIX, Dec., 1949.

Price. P.H. and Woodward H.P., Geology and War, New Jerssey, 1832.

INDEX